THE
WAY
THINGS
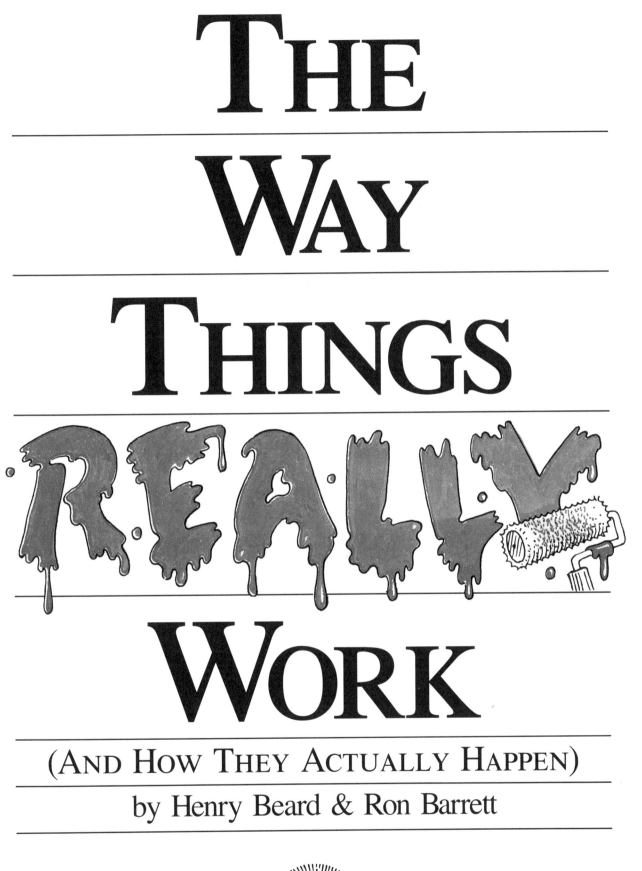
REALLY
WORK

(AND HOW THEY ACTUALLY HAPPEN)

by Henry Beard & Ron Barrett

VIKING

Vɪκɪɴɢ
Published by the Penguin Group
Penguin Books USA Inc., 375 Hudson Street,
New York, New York 10014, U.S.A.
Penguin Books Ltd, 27 Wrights Lane,
London W8 5TZ, England
Penguin Books Australia Ltd, Ringwood,
Victoria, Australia
Penguin Books Canada Ltd, 10 Alcorn Avenue,
Toronto, Ontario, Canada M4V 3B2
Penguin Books (N.Z.) Ltd, 182–190 Wairau Road,
Auckland 10, New Zealand

Penguin Books Ltd, Registered Offices:
Harmondsworth, Middlesex, England

First published in 1993 by Viking Penguin,
a division of Penguin Books USA Inc.

10 9 8 7 6 5 4 3 2 1

Copyright © Ron Barrett, John Boswell, and Henry Beard, 1993
All rights reserved

ISBN 0-670-85073-X

CIP data available

Printed in the United States of America
Set in Times Roman
Designed by Ron Barrett

TABLE OF CONTENTS

INTRODUCTION

If you're one of those people who sits in a plane pondering the principles of jet propulsion, or stands in an elevator and tries to visualize the complex system of cables, pulleys, and counterweights that whisks you from floor to floor, or looks at a snapshot and imagines the amazing chemical process that makes an image appear on a blank strip of film, put this book down right now and buy a copy of David Macaulay's brilliant guide to the workings of machines, *The Way Things Work*.

If, on the other hand, you're the kind of person who sits on that plane brooding over the fact that your luggage, which you watched being tagged for Denver, is going to end up in the airport in Tegucigalpa, Honduras, or who stands there trying to figure out how the elevator you just missed knew to close its doors in your face, or who wonders why the pictures you take are always blurry and tilted and make everyone look fifty pounds fatter, then *The Way Things Really Work* is the book for you.

Now, you've probably always believed that these and dozens of other daily examples of technology gone haywire are the result of some supernatural force or mysterious effect, like gremlins or Murphy's Laws, but the fact is that just as the functioning of planes, and elevators, and cameras, and other 20th-century marvels is governed by the basic laws of physics, mechanics, and optics, and not—as children sometimes think—by magic, so too is their apparent malfunctioning.

Of course, the key word here is *apparent,* because if only someone would sketch out for you the inner workings of these puzzling mechanisms and let you peer inside the hidden structure of these bewildering systems, you'd see in a flash that they aren't malfunctioning at all—they are things of beauty, performing their assigned tasks to absolute perfection.

And that is exactly what *The Way Things Really Work* does for you. Here, depicted in scores of thoroughly researched and precisely detailed illustrations are all the ingenious devices and inventive designs that are responsible for the countless inconveniences of our modern world—everything from minor annoyances like hair-trigger car alarms, unstartable lawn mowers, and coin-devouring candy machines, to major aggravations like traffic jams, nuclear power, and the Pentagon.

We realize that it may be difficult to accept the awful truth that the overwhelming majority of the products and processes of our sophisticated civilization has been deliberately created to frustrate, exasperate, and infuriate the largest possible number of people, but as you peruse the hundreds of revealing drawings in these pages, it will quickly become clear to you that there is no other credible explanation for the perverse behavior of gizmos as small as the pocket knives that nick us and the shower fixtures that scald us to institutions as huge as that ultimate symbol of programmed ineptitude, the government of the United States.

Yes, we know what you're going to say. If we had the national will and technical expertise to send men to the moon, why couldn't we design something as simple as an airline luggage-handling system that actually sends baggage to the same place as its owners?

Well, in a way, a little-known photograph, one of thousands from the last Apollo mission, provides an ironic answer. Taken by a robot camera as the lunar module blasts off, and transmitted back to earth, it shows the abandoned moon buggy, the obligatory flag, some pieces of discarded equipment, and in the corner of the image, silhouetted against the deeply cratered landscape, three matching pieces of pale blue Samsonite luggage. The PanAm tags for Miami airport fastened to their handles are clearly legible in the eerie glare.

HENRY BEARD AND RON BARRETT

How Candy Machines Eat Your Quarters

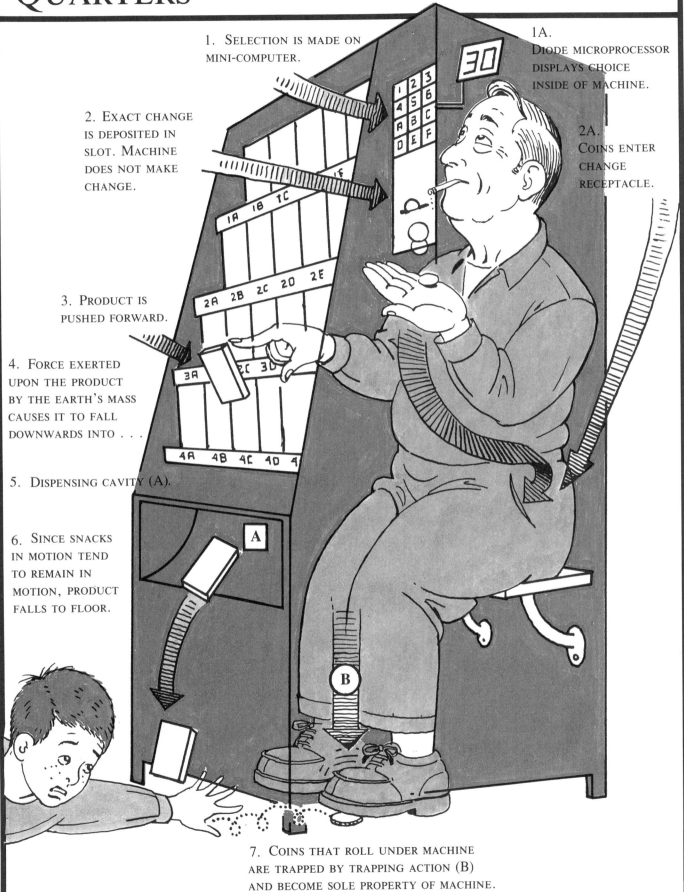

1. Selection is made on mini-computer.

1A. Diode microprocessor displays choice inside of machine.

2. Exact change is deposited in slot. Machine does not make change.

2A. Coins enter change receptacle.

3. Product is pushed forward.

4. Force exerted upon the product by the earth's mass causes it to fall downwards into . . .

5. Dispensing cavity (A).

6. Since snacks in motion tend to remain in motion, product falls to floor.

7. Coins that roll under machine are trapped by trapping action (B) and become sole property of machine.

How Airlines Lose Your Luggage

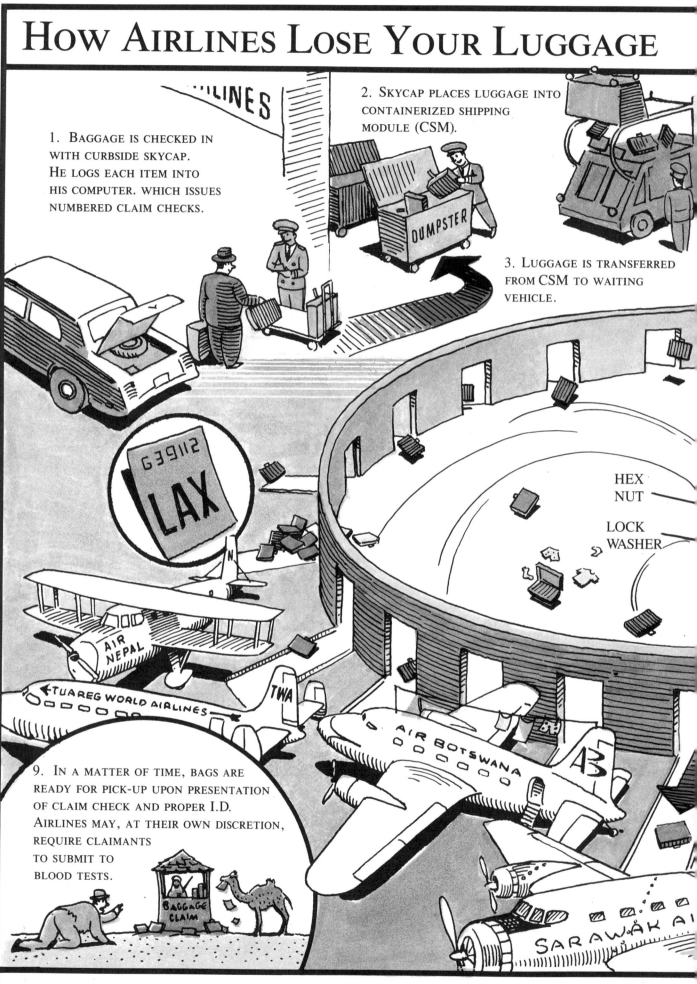

1. Baggage is checked in with curbside skycap. He logs each item into his computer. which issues numbered claim checks.

2. Skycap places luggage into containerized shipping module (CSM).

3. Luggage is transferred from CSM to waiting vehicle.

HEX NUT

LOCK WASHER

9. In a matter of time, bags are ready for pick-up upon presentation of claim check and proper I.D. Airlines may, at their own discretion, require claimants to submit to blood tests.

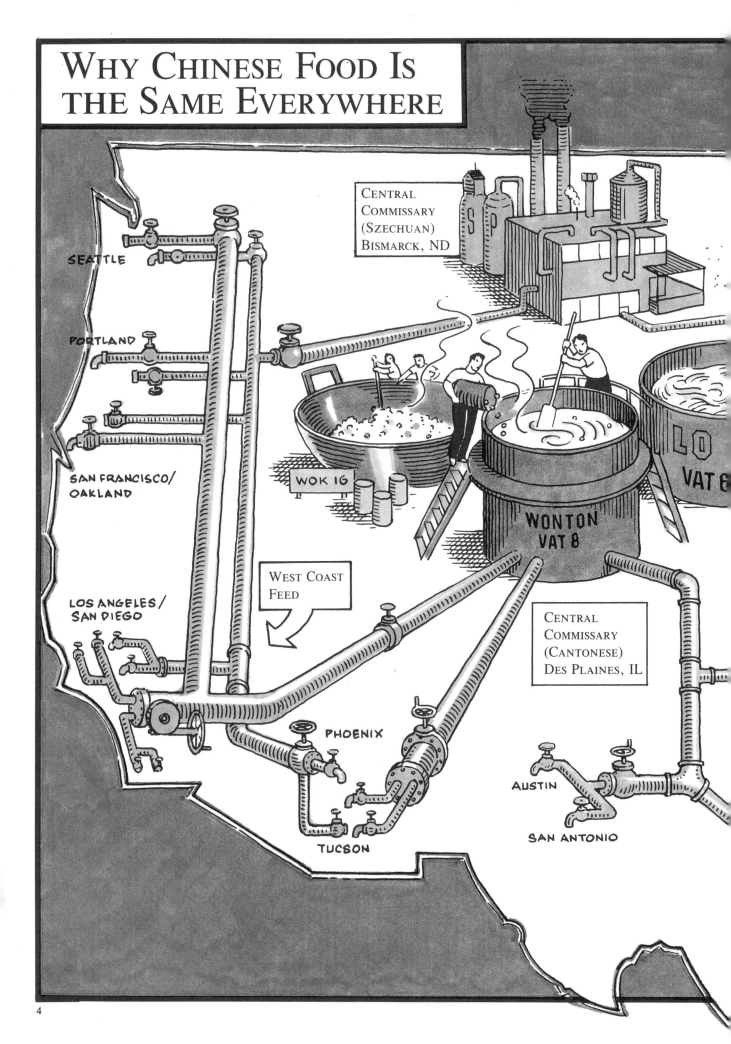

WHY CHINESE FOOD IS THE SAME EVERYWHERE

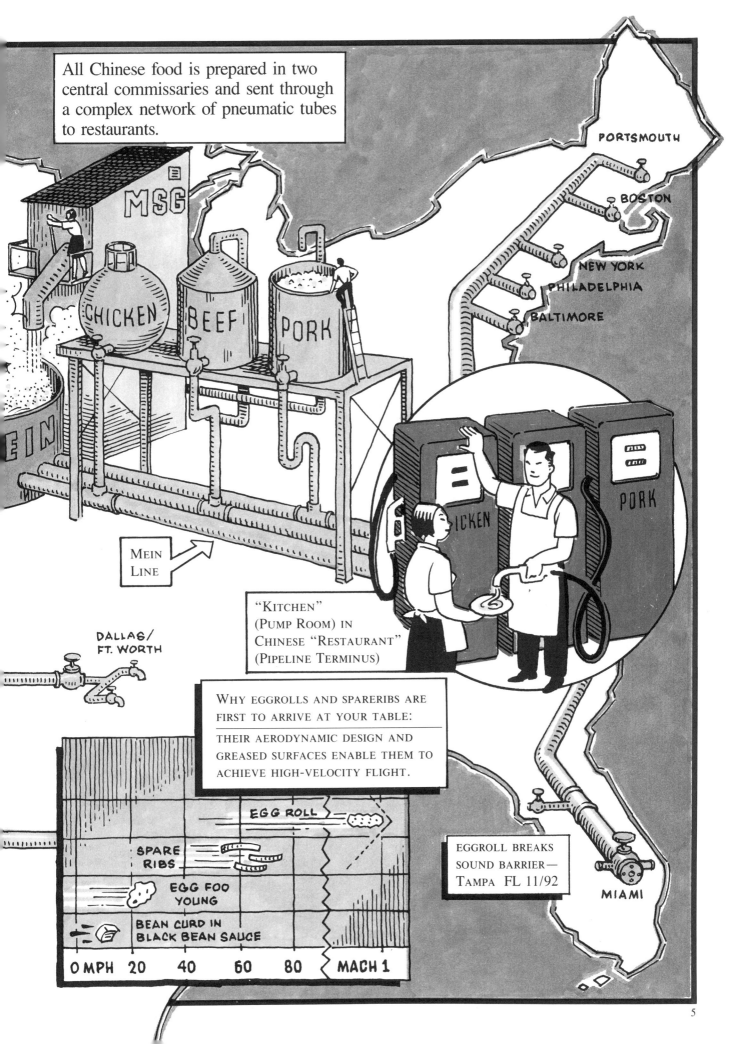

All Chinese food is prepared in two central commissaries and sent through a complex network of pneumatic tubes to restaurants.

PORTSMOUTH

BOSTON

NEW YORK

PHILADELPHIA

BALTIMORE

MSG

CHICKEN

BEEF

PORK

EIN

MEIN LINE

DALLAS/ FT. WORTH

"KITCHEN" (PUMP ROOM) IN CHINESE "RESTAURANT" (PIPELINE TERMINUS)

ICKEN

PORK

WHY EGGROLLS AND SPARERIBS ARE FIRST TO ARRIVE AT YOUR TABLE:

THEIR AERODYNAMIC DESIGN AND GREASED SURFACES ENABLE THEM TO ACHIEVE HIGH-VELOCITY FLIGHT.

EGGROLL BREAKS SOUND BARRIER— TAMPA FL 11/92

MIAMI

EGG ROLL

SPARE RIBS

EGG FOO YOUNG

BEAN CURD IN BLACK BEAN SAUCE

| 0 MPH | 20 | 40 | 60 | 80 | MACH 1 |

Why Announcements in Train Stations and Bus Terminals Are Incomprehensible

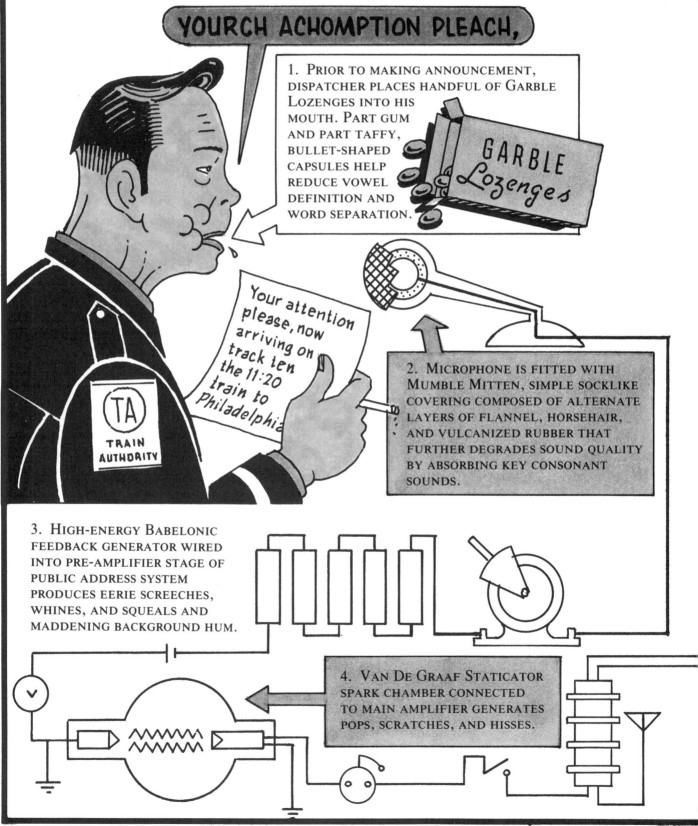

Why Lawn Mowers Are So Hard to Start

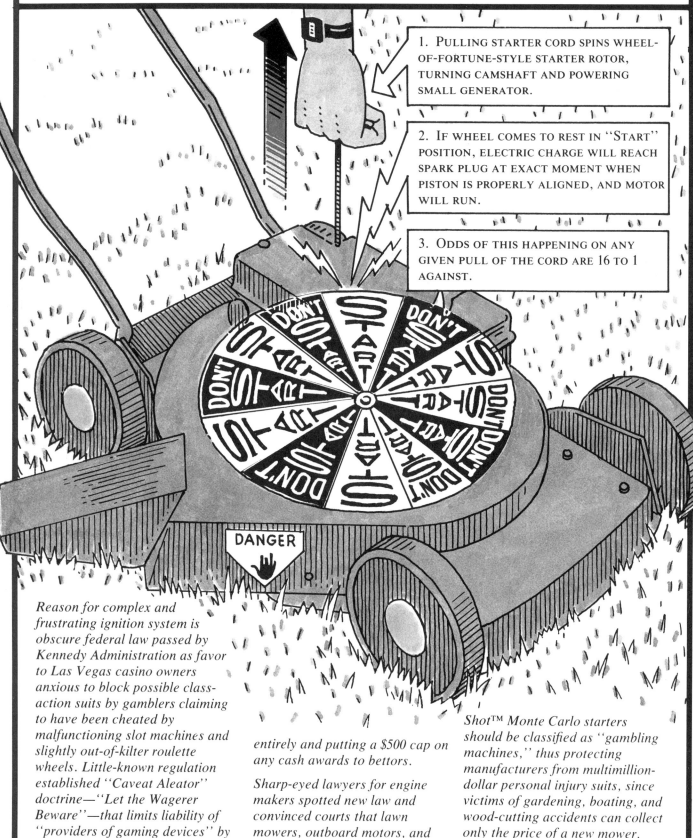

1. Pulling starter cord spins wheel-of-fortune-style starter rotor, turning camshaft and powering small generator.

2. If wheel comes to rest in "Start" position, electric charge will reach spark plug at exact moment when piston is properly aligned, and motor will run.

3. Odds of this happening on any given pull of the cord are 16 to 1 against.

DANGER

Reason for complex and frustrating ignition system is obscure federal law passed by Kennedy Administration as favor to Las Vegas casino owners anxious to block possible class-action suits by gamblers claiming to have been cheated by malfunctioning slot machines and slightly out-of-kilter roulette wheels. Little-known regulation established "Caveat Aleator" doctrine—"Let the Wagerer Beware"—that limits liability of "providers of gaming devices" by eliminating punitive damages

entirely and putting a $500 cap on any cash awards to bettors.

Sharp-eyed lawyers for engine makers spotted new law and convinced courts that lawn mowers, outboard motors, and chainsaws with patented Long-

Shot™ Monte Carlo starters should be classified as "gambling machines," thus protecting manufacturers from multimillion-dollar personal injury suits, since victims of gardening, boating, and wood-cutting accidents can collect only the price of a new mower, motor, or saw.

Why Toast Always Lands Jelly Side Down

Using same 2-billion-dollar supercomputer at Department of Agriculture recently employed in 10-year effort to determine which came first, chicken or egg (results are classified), scientists at Bureau of Breakfast Affairs studied three basic "burdened-bread" descent modes—"Hand Bobble," "Plate Slide," and "Blade Flip"— to pinpoint exact reason why toast-drops always have "worst-case outcomes."

I. HAND BOBBLE

1. *Temporary loss of toast control during transfer to plate following jelly application elicits reflexive muscular overreaction. Abrupt upward movement of palm to reestablish positive hand/bread contact instead provides motive force to launch toast.*

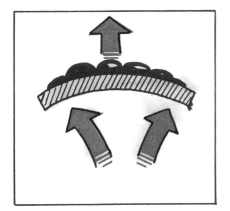

2. *Greater specific gravity of dense jelly mass in relation to light, air-filled toasted bread slice induces toast to curve into convex shape as it travels upward.*

REFLEX POINT

3. *When toast reaches apogee of its trajectory, effect is sharply reversed. Bread now bends into concave shape, but unevenness of jelly distribution on toast surface results in off-center reflex point that deflects toast out of horizontal descent plane.*

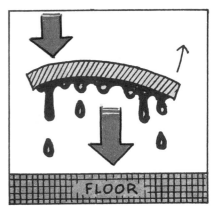

FLOOR

4. *Once this unbalanced recoil is initiated, it continues until overturning motion of jelly-laden surface is halted by contact with kitchen floor.*

II. PLATE SLIDE

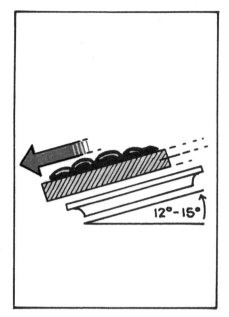

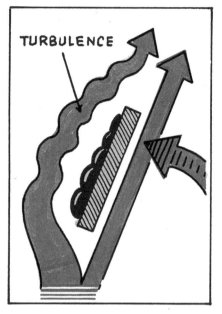

1. *Toast begins to slide when Critical Slide Angle is reached—between 12° and 15° of plate-tip, depending on dish type, depth of rim, surface characteristics, etc.*

2. *Air passing over raised jelly surface has further to travel than air passing beneath smooth underslice area. Pressure differential produces strong airplane-wing-type lift effect.*

3. *Fractal nature of jelly surface causes turbulence, which dissipates lifting force and shifts center of effective mass to trailing edge of bread. Since initial angle of attack was steep, toast quickly "stalls" and begins to nose-dive.*

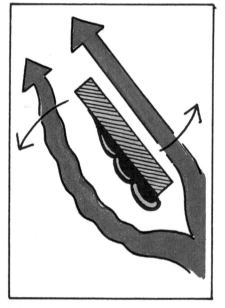

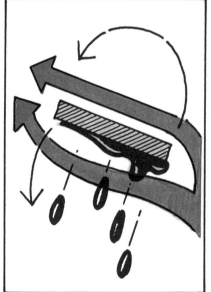

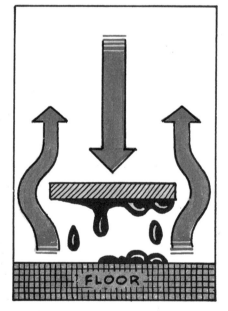

4. *Jelly flows forward in response to gravity, and shift in distribution of weight coupled with off-center axis of rotation triggers sudden "kick-over," reversing plane of toast descent.*

5. *As jelly blobs begin to drop to floor from edge of toast, turnover motion is magnified by rapid lightening of crust-edge load and momentary decrease in drag over somewhat smoother, partially dejellied surface.*

6. *Effect is completed when crust edges stabilize airflow in inverted horizontal position, and weight of remaining jelly pulls jelly side of toast slice directly toward floor.*

III. BLADE FLIP

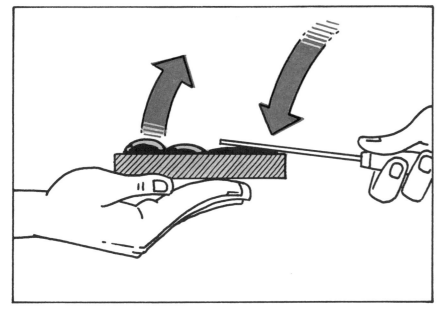

1. *Pressure of jelly knife on excessively cantilevered toast slice leads to classic tiddlywink flip.*

2. *Kinetic energy of flip propels toast outward and upward and imparts powerful end-over-end rotation.*

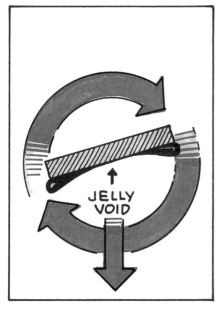

3. *Centrifugal force generated by axial motion sends jelly out toward crust edges, creating telltale "jelly void" in center of toast surface.*

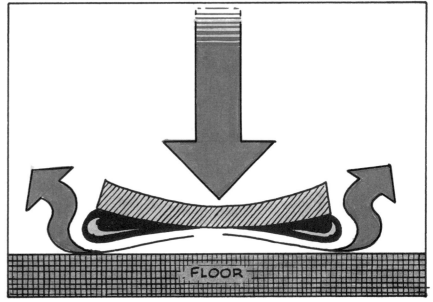

4. *As law of conservation of angular momentum slows tumbling, vacuum resulting from laminar air flow through jelly void creates suction effect, producing distinct "smok" sound when jelly meets floor.*

HOW INSTRUCTIONS FOR VCRs, MICROWAVES, AND OTHER ELECTRONIC PRODUCTS ARE WRITTEN

1. STEP-BY-STEP DESCRIPTION OF BASIC FEATURES OF PRODUCT AND METHOD OF OPERATION IS WRITTEN IN CLEAR JAPANESE BY A TEAM OF TECHNICAL WRITERS AND PRODUCT ENGINEERS.

2. THEIR WORK IS TRANSMITTED OVERSEAS, WHERE IT IS TRANSLATED INTO A "NEUTRAL TRANSITION LANGUAGE," USUALLY DANISH.

3. RESULTING TEXT IS READ BY A NON-DANISH SPEAKER TO ANOTHER NON-DANISH SPEAKER OVER PAYPHONES IN A TRAIN STATION.

4. THIS "BASIC OPERATING TEXT" IS THEN TRANSLATED INTO ENGLISH, FRENCH, GERMAN, SPANISH, AND ITALIAN AND ANY OTHER DESIRED LANGUAGE BY STUDENTS AT A LANGUAGE SCHOOL IN INDONESIA WORKING UNDER LONG-TERM CONTRACT TO JAPANESE ELECTRONICS INDUSTRY.

5. FINAL VERSION IS CHECKED FOR INCOMPREHENSIBILITY BY ORIGINAL ENGINEERING AND DESIGN TEAM.

How Elevators Know to Close Their Doors When You Come Running

Elevators are equipped with two distinct automatic sensors that control opening and closing of doors. First is familiar "electric eye," a photoelectric cell located between inner and outer doors that keeps them from closing when entering or departing passenger breaks light beam.

Second sensor—an audioelectric cell or "electric ear"—is designed to slam the elevator doors shut whenever anyone hurries to enter car. Usually mounted behind direction indicator above hoistway portal, sensitive sound detector is programmed to respond to distinct clatter of rapidly approaching heels by immediately triggering a high-speed hydraulic closing lever. Pressure-sensitive mats may also be used in buildings where carpeting in hallways muffles the footfalls of approaching prospective passengers.

INDICATOR SENSOR

PISTON

CLACK!

CLICK!

PRESSURE
SENSITIVE MAT
UNDER CARPETING

WHY FLASHLIGHTS NEVER WORK

Although the basic design of tube flashlights seems simple and trouble-free, they are all subject to a complex phenomenon called "proximity induction" that occurs whenever a switch and a bulb are located very close to a primary power source.

This baffling force basically overrides simple on-off function of thumb switch, transforming it into a "dynamic flux circuit" with a theoretically infinite number of "wave states," but as a practical matter, flashlights usually end up with only 8 possible switch positions.

1. ON
2. OFF
3. ON-OFF-OFF-OFF-ON
4. OFF-OFF-ON-OFF
5. ON IF YOU SHAKE IT
6. OFF IF YOU HOLD IT LEVEL
7. ON IF YOU BANG IT HARD ENOUGH TO CRACK THE LENS, THEN WON'T TURN OFF UNLESS DISASSEMBLED
8. ON-OFF-ON WEAKLY-OFF-ON BRIGHTLY-OFF FOREVER

FEEBLE GLOW

BULB

PRIMARY POWER SOURCE

THUMB SWITCH

SPRING

NORTH-SOUTH BATTERY   EAST-WEST BATTERY

Many batteries marked with negative and positive signs indicating "north-south" polarities are mislabelled. In fact, about a third of all batteries are naturally "east-west" with "indecisive" and "tentative" poles. When placed in contact with incompatible cells, they quickly lose their charge.

MAGNETIC FIELD

About 10 minutes after flashlight is set down lens-first on flat surface, well-known electroperpendicular effect begins to operate, gradually establishing a magnetic field that bypasses switch, turning bulb on. Light is not visible, so batteries are depleted before anyone notices.

How Car Alarms Work

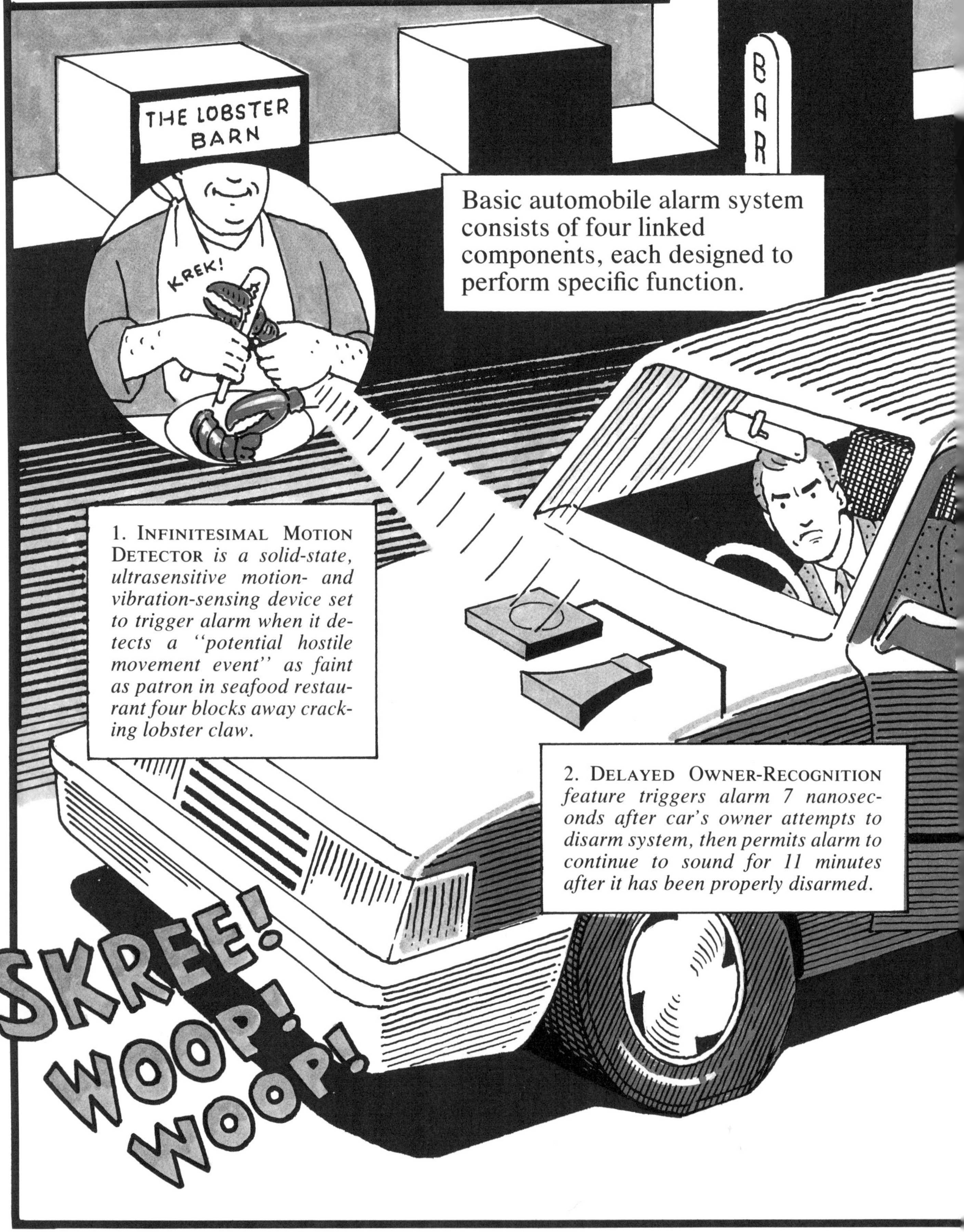

3. HIGH-IMPACT OVERRIDE *circuitry instantly cancels alarm-triggering mechanism if car window is struck with sledgehammer, door is violently pried open with crowbar, screwdriver is inserted in any of its locks, or vehicle is driven away by unauthorized driver.*

4. DISTANCE-VARIABLE MULTI-PITCH DOPPLER-FREQUENCY SHIFT ANTAGONIZER SIREN *produces remarkably sophisticated "acoustical product" or noise that actually causes more pain and distress the farther it travels from source.*

Within 10 meters (30 feet) of car, the mind-unhinging wail is exactly cancelled by precisely phase-matched sine-reversed sound damper that bathes potential thief or vandal in a soothing low hum, but from 100 meters out (about 120 yards) sonic masking effect dissipates rapidly, and underlying 155-decibel randomly warbling wail does not reach maximum intensity until it travels 3 kilometers (2 miles) from source, at which point it has equivalent sound energy of a fingernail 50 meters long (160 ft.) and 10 centimeters thick (4 inches) scraping down a giant blackboard.

HOTEL

3k

100m

10m

HUM

155 db

Why You Can't Ever Remember Anybody's Name

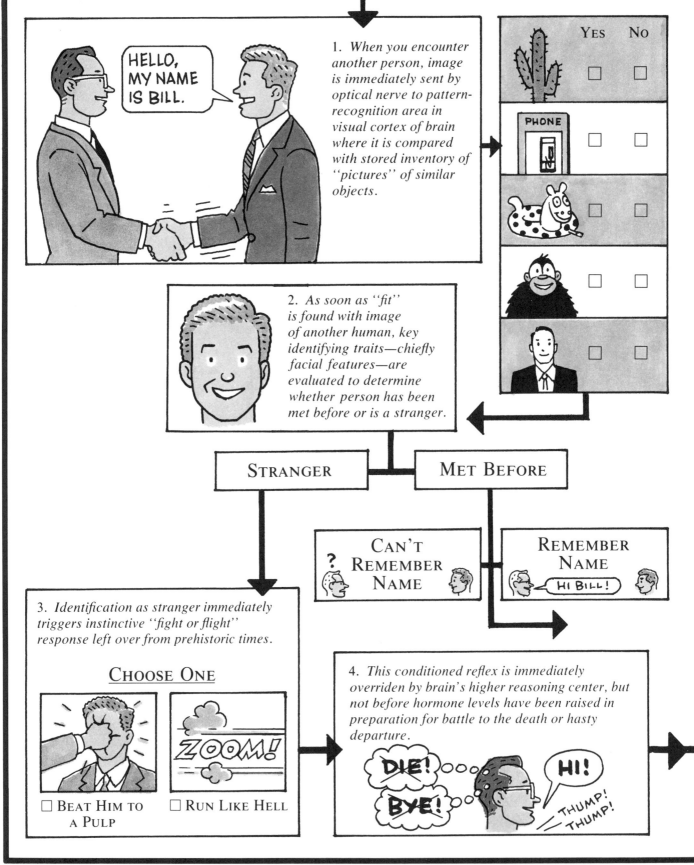

5. When stranger gives his name, it is sent by way of auditory nerve to parts of brain dedicated to speech-recognition and language-formation.

HELLO, MY NAME IS BILL

6. These little-understood zones in forebrain process incoming sounds according to wide variety of possible categories and interpretations.

NAMES THAT SOUND LIKE 'ILL'	POSSIBLE MEANINGS OF "BILL"	LETTERS B-I-L-L IN SAME ORDER, SORT OF
PHIL	DEBT RECORD	
WILL		HILLBILLY
JILL	BANK NOTE	BILLYGOAT
GIL	CAP VISOR	BILLIONS
BILL		BOUILLON CUBE
	DUCK SNOUT	
		BRILLO
	THIS GUY	

7. At the same time, stranger's face is added to thousands of others from previous meetings and introductions.

BILL   WHOSIS   WHATSERNAME   WHATSHISFACE

8. Increased sensitivity to sound and movement produced by original release of hormones, together with any special effort to concentrate on name, prime memory to absorb any simultaneously occurring auditory stimuli.

IT'S A BULL MARKET BUD-STAND PAT.

JOE JUST BOUGHT A BOBSLED TOM.

SAM, I'LL BE FRANK WITH YOU.

I WAS AT THE GYM WITH TED.

BACK IN A JIFFY, JEFF. I'VE GOT TO GO TO THE JOHN.

HELLO, MY NAME IS BILL.

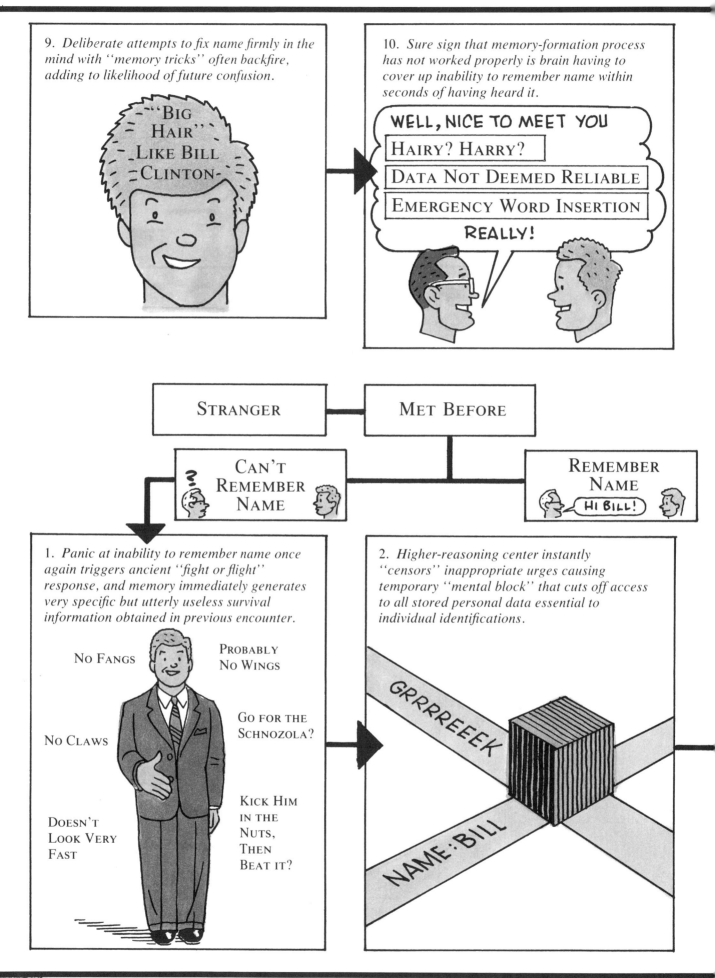

3. *When normal flow of stream of consciousness along cerebral networks is restored, dammed-up flood of recollections is suddenly released in huge rush of unorganized details.*

4. *Unable to recognize key information being sought against background clutter of neural impulses, brain rejects all of them, producing classic "my mind is a total blank" feeling.*

5. *Fortunately, odds are excellent that person whose name you can't remember has forgotten yours, too.*

How to Use a Pasta-Making Machine

1.

Make pasta dough. Be sure to follow recipe in pasta machine instruction book to the letter—amounts and types of ingredients must be exactly those called for.

2.

Work dough ball carefully. Too little kneading makes it crumbly; too much handling makes it tough.

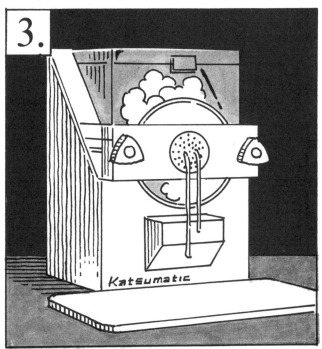

3.

Place dough in machine, adjust setting for desired shape and width of pasta, and turn machine on.

4.

As pasta emerges from nozzle, catch limp ribbons of dough in hands, cut in 12-inch lengths, and drape over everything in sight.

5. Put pasta in boiling water. Cook for 45 seconds, then serve.

6. Suggested recipes: Knottuchine Alfredo, Snafucci Carbonara, Tangliateri Bolognese.

7. Get out stool. Open door of unreachable cabinet above refrigerator. Make space by pushing ice cream maker, electric mixer, pressure cooker, and waffle iron further back. Put pasta machine in cabinet.

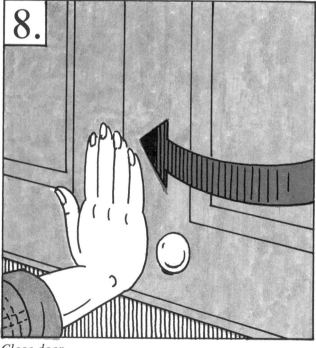

8. Close door.

WHAT HAPPENS WHEN YOU VOTE

Voters often wonder why operation of huge hard-to-move lever is necessary to record vote on mechanical voting machines.

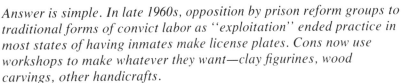

Answer is simple. In late 1960s, opposition by prison reform groups to traditional forms of convict labor as "exploitation" ended practice in most states of having inmates make license plates. Cons now use workshops to make whatever they want—clay figurines, wood carvings, other handicrafts.

At the same time, newer, lighter aluminum alloys transformed metal stamping, and odorless super-fast chromo-gel cold-color plastic paint did away with need for messy, smelly sprays and high-temperature enamel-baking process. Obvious solution was to have citizens manufacture license plates when they vote.

Bulky cabinet of voting machine houses roll of license plate blanks prepainted with background color, adjustable wheels with die-cut faces for numbers and letters, and simple hand-operated stamping press.

When lever is pulled to left, curtain closes, next plate blank is moved into position, and number and letter wheels are advanced. Flicking little switches by names of candidates does nothing, but when lever is pushed to right, plate is cut from roll, stamped, and imprinted with second and third colors on raised numbers and letters. Telltale "clunk" is sound of finished plate dropping onto stack.

Even though voter turnout is low, large number of elections—federal, state, local—and greater durability of plates combine to satisfy need easily. When day's totals are tallied, only license plates are counted, since machine does not register votes. Election results are determined by computers using averages of most recent TV polls percentages, which are applied to plate production figures to calculate actual turnout and final vote totals.

HOW TRAFFIC JAMS HAPPEN

Although minor traffic tie-ups are usually result of chance—accidents and rubbernecking, weather conditions, holiday rushes, and so on—mammoth area-wide stoppages require considerable planning.

Speed-reduction specialists study list of budgeted highway improvement and repair projects. Essential work usually supplies key elements of "Flow Restriction Plan," or FRP, but frivolous undertakings, such as planting flowers in median strips, renumbering light poles, and sandblasting historic markers, are always included to supply needed flexibility.

Computers are used to simulate effect of simultaneous lane closures and traffic diversions at key chokepoints, but congestion creation is an art, and bottleneck experts, or "jam masters" (or simply "jammers"), rely on feel developed over years of causing commuting nightmares to decide where to place telltale orange cones for key "choke test" that precedes every major transportation disruption.

Data gathered from results of temporary detours set up in as many as a dozen widely separated locations is evaluated, and Traffic Obstruction Team makes final decision on precise spots to deploy hundreds of dump trucks, bulldozers, pavers, sandblasters, bucket loaders, and cranes at their command.

Often many weeks, even months, of preparation have gone into "Jam Plan" covering as much as 100 square miles, but it all comes down to a few simple words from a guy in a helicopter.

THE WAY PETS REALLY WORK: HOW A $3 GOLDFISH CAN MAKE YOU SPEND $50 BY DYING

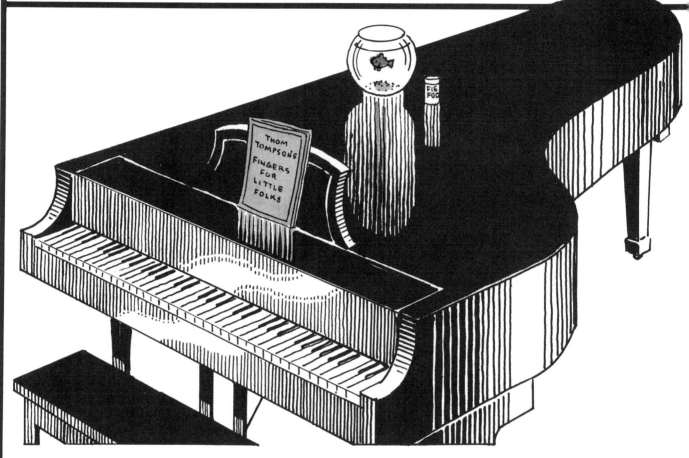

Your child wants an Irish Setter as a pet. After intense negotiations, child agrees to goldfish.

Fish's water must be nonchlorinated.

Fish has 48-hour warranty. At end of 48th hour fish rolls on its side, breathes weakly, and lifts its eyes heavenward. Child manifests extreme anxiety. Fish is rushed back to pet store for diagnosis: "Swim Bladder Infection." Store employee says medicine must be administered in a tank with circulating, filtered water.

FOOD: $1.29
BOWL: $7.25
GRAVEL: $2.98
PRICE OF GOLDFISH: $3.00
1 GAL. SPRING WATER: $1.25

MEDICINE: $5.95
PUMP: $9.99
FILTER: $7.00

Pump and medicine are put in bowl. Fish is spun as in blender on "Puree." Fish must have large tank.

Pet store employee unwilling to give assurance of fish's survival. Fish dies next day.

Child takes news calmly. Says "Never liked goldfish anyway." Child now wants more than one fish for backup when death occurs.

Neon Tetras are tropical fish requiring water temperature of 70°F.

Tank looks empty without plastic plant, bubbling skull, and backdrop of lost continent, Atlantis.

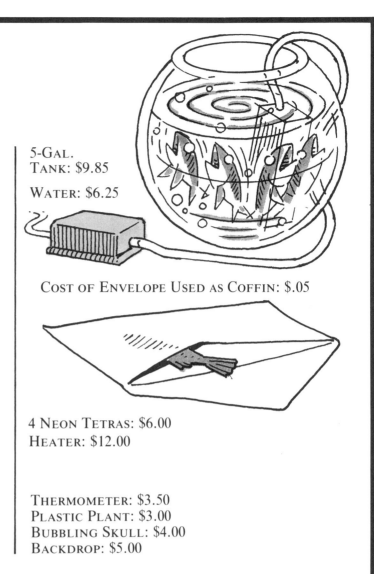

5-GAL. TANK: $9.85

WATER: $6.25

COST OF ENVELOPE USED AS COFFIN: $.05

4 NEON TETRAS: $6.00
HEATER: $12.00

THERMOMETER: $3.50
PLASTIC PLANT: $3.00
BUBBLING SKULL: $4.00
BACKDROP: $5.00

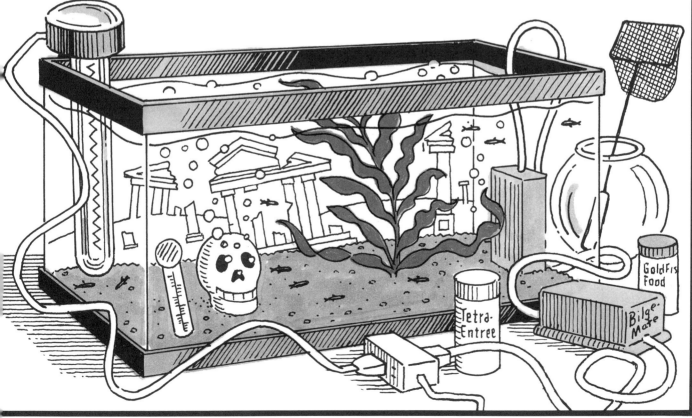

WHY YOU ONLY LIKE FOODS THAT ARE BAD FOR YOU AND MAKE YOU FAT

PREFERENCES FOR CERTAIN FOODS AND AVERSIONS TO OTHERS ARE RESULT OF MILLIONS OF YEARS OF EVOLUTION.

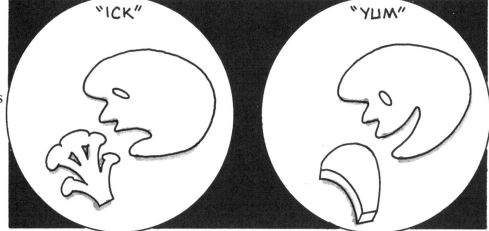

STRUGGLE FOR SURVIVAL CAUSED OUR EARLIEST HUMAN ANCESTORS TO REJECT DIET OF SHRUBS AND GRASSES IN FAVOR OF ONE RICH IN EASILY STORED, HIGH-ENERGY FATS AND SUGARS.

THUS, IN MODERN MAN, SENSE OF TASTE IS PRIMARILY TRIGGERED BY CALORIES—NO CALORIES, NO TASTE.

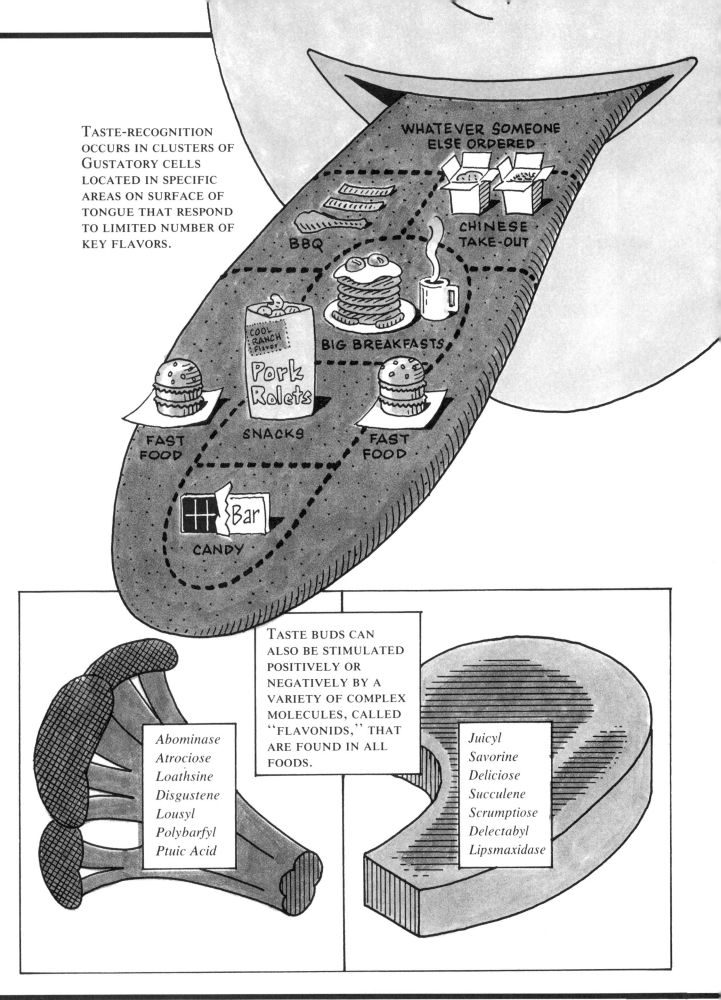

TASTE-RECOGNITION OCCURS IN CLUSTERS OF GUSTATORY CELLS LOCATED IN SPECIFIC AREAS ON SURFACE OF TONGUE THAT RESPOND TO LIMITED NUMBER OF KEY FLAVORS.

WHATEVER SOMEONE ELSE ORDERED

CHINESE TAKE-OUT

BBQ

BIG BREAKFASTS

FAST FOOD

SNACKS

FAST FOOD

CANDY

TASTE BUDS CAN ALSO BE STIMULATED POSITIVELY OR NEGATIVELY BY A VARIETY OF COMPLEX MOLECULES, CALLED "FLAVONIDS," THAT ARE FOUND IN ALL FOODS.

Abominase
Atrociose
Loathsine
Disgustene
Lousyl
Polybarfyl
Ptuic Acid

Juicyl
Savorine
Deliciose
Succulene
Scrumptiose
Delectabyl
Lipsmaxidase

PERSONAL LIKES AND DISLIKES ARE
PROGRAMMED INTO DNA OF OUR
INDIVIDUAL GENES, BUT ALL FOLLOW
BASIC PATTERN OF HUMAN DIET
SELECTION.

UNLESS GENETIC ENGINEERING
SUCCEEDS IN ALTERING FUNDAMENTAL
STRUCTURE OF HUMAN GENOME, LASTING
CHANGE IN OUR DIETS IS UNLIKELY TO
TAKE PLACE.

How the Pentagon Spends a Million Dollars a Minute

Individual Hand-Held Arm-Activated Man-Portable Radar-Evading Reduced-Visibility Optically Targeted Direct-Impact Generator and Fulcrum-Force-Transfer Tool—M119A1, Stealth Hammer

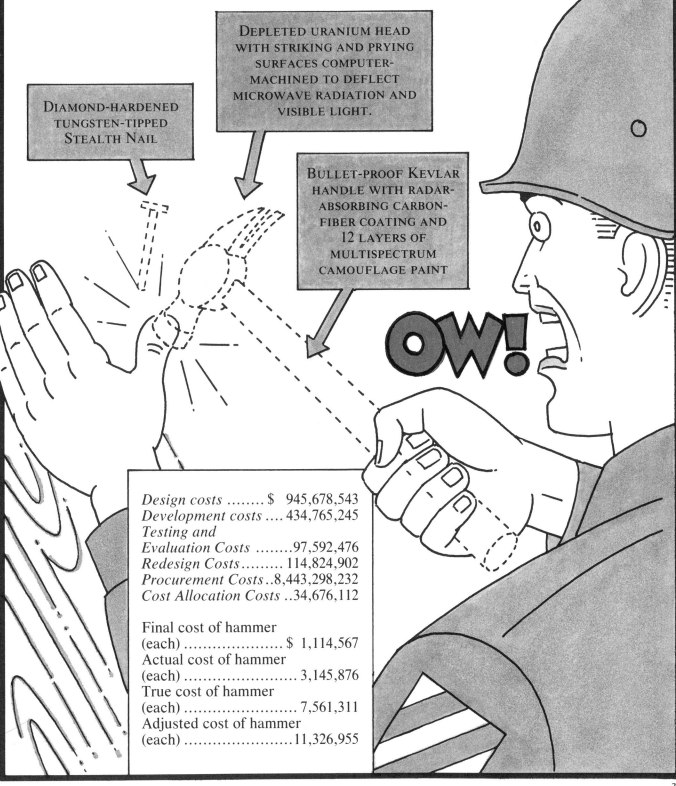

How Hotel Bath and Shower Fixtures Were Designed

1. *All known methods of regulating flow and adjusting temperature of fluids are studied.*

2. *Mock-ups of designs judged to be practical for adaptation to shower use but whose function is not immediately apparent are constructed. Tests are conducted using undergraduates at M.I.T. and Caltech. Any of the devices whose basic operation could be grasped within ten minutes are immediately discarded.*

3. *Prototypes of promising designs are fabricated and installed in several prisons to be tested by inmates participating in early-release programs. Designs not destroyed within a week are rejected.*

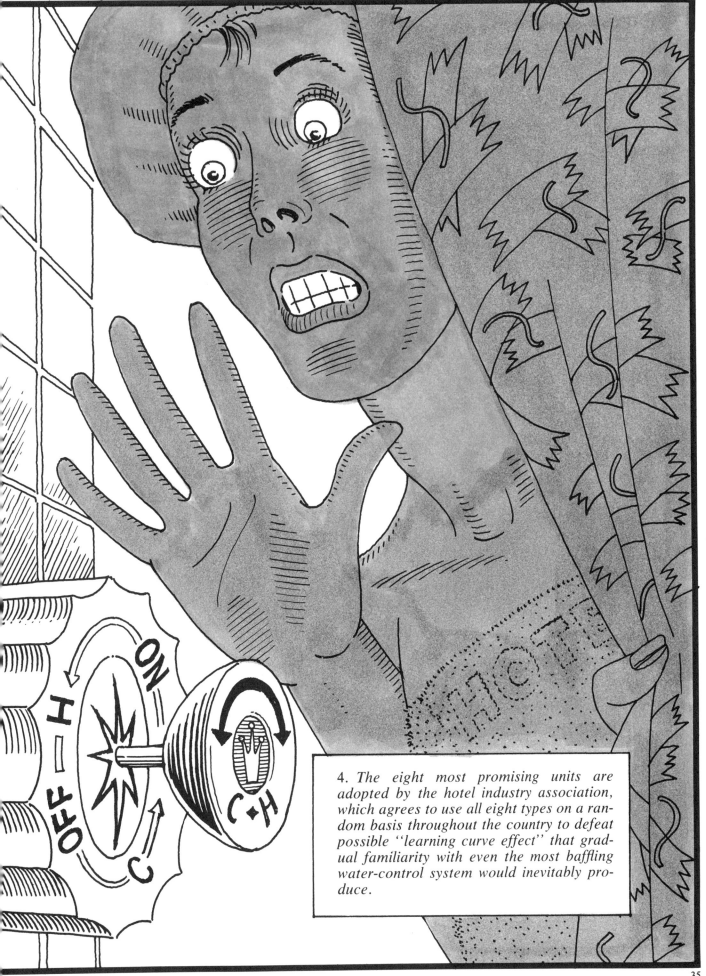

4. The eight most promising units are adopted by the hotel industry association, which agrees to use all eight types on a random basis throughout the country to defeat possible "learning curve effect" that gradual familiarity with even the most baffling water-control system would inevitably produce.

DAY 2

4. *He/she brings your mail to the post office and the sharing continues.*

5. *The mail is sorted . . .*

7. *and bagged.*

6. *cancelled . . .*

DAY 6

13. *Letter carrier, recovering from sick day, is not up to demanding task of precisely matching addresses on envelopes with house numbers and leaves letters with neighbor.*

DAYS 7, 8, 9

14. *Neighbor puts your mail with a stack of bills. Forgets about it.*

DAY 10

15. *Your electricity is disconnected. Neighbor brings over flashlight and misdelivered letters, among which is bill threatening disconnection for nonpayment.*

HOW ZAMBONIS WORK

Left to right: Rosa Zamboni, Maria Zamboni, Sophia Zamboni

HOW TO READ A FRENCH WINE LABEL

Old French proverb among wine makers, "Le dessin revèle le raisin" ("The label betrays the grape"), refers to long-standing habit of French vintners of quietly signaling quality of each year's production to fellow citizens without hurting overseas sales. Concealed on labels among familiar details about region, type of wine, vintage, classification of growth, and so on are four basic kinds of secret information.

FENESTRATION

Count number of windows in little drawing of château on label. Even number of windows = good year; odd number = rotten year.

COMPOSITION

On labels with no little château, check placement of year of vintage on label. If year is above center, wine is lousy. Remember: "Year on top, wine is slop."

Grand Vin de Bretagne

1984

APPELATION SAINT-MALO CONTROLÉE

MIS EN BOUTEILLES AU CHATEAU

Ste Cie des Vignobles de la Manche

PROPRIÉTAIRE À DINAN (CÔTES-DU-NORD)

FRANCE

12% VOL.   75 CL.

CONFIGURATION

Labels themselves fall into three categories of shapes that show which market wine was produced for. Key to meaning of shapes:

Wine for consumption in France

Wine for export and cooking

Wine for gifts and for serving at large parties

METRICATION

Contents of typical full bottle are measured in parts of liter—either 75 cl (centiliters) or 750 ml (milliliters). Although amounts are identical, choice of metric unit is not accidental, but private prediction by wine maker as to whether wine will be any good after a few years in cellar. Memory aid: cl = "Can't Last"; ml = "Might Last."

How to Eat with Chopsticks

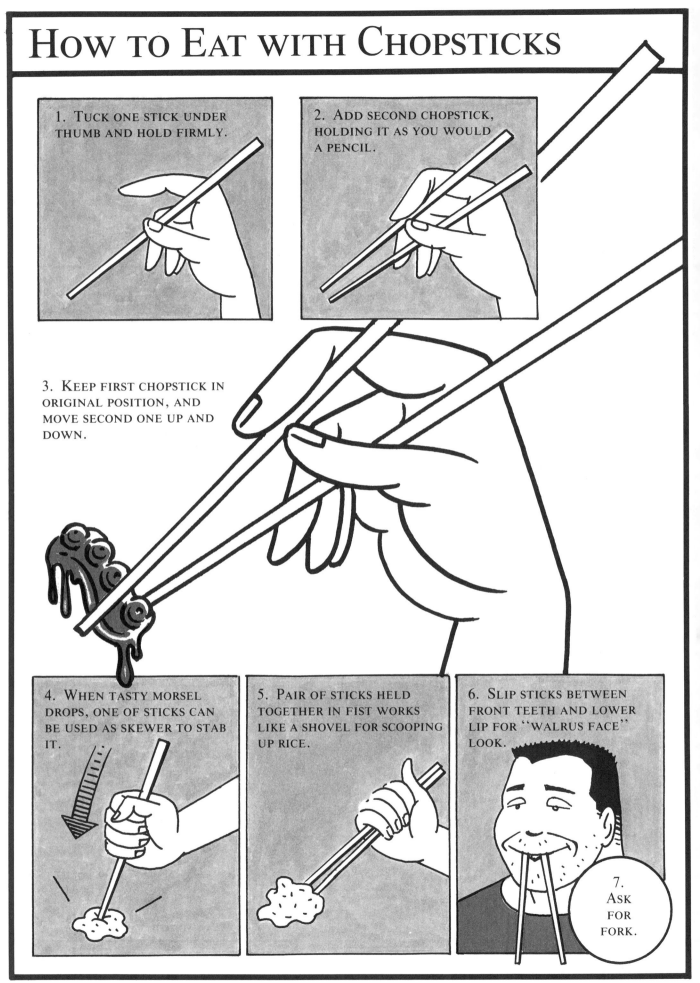

1. TUCK ONE STICK UNDER THUMB AND HOLD FIRMLY.

2. ADD SECOND CHOPSTICK, HOLDING IT AS YOU WOULD A PENCIL.

3. KEEP FIRST CHOPSTICK IN ORIGINAL POSITION, AND MOVE SECOND ONE UP AND DOWN.

4. WHEN TASTY MORSEL DROPS, ONE OF STICKS CAN BE USED AS SKEWER TO STAB IT.

5. PAIR OF STICKS HELD TOGETHER IN FIST WORKS LIKE A SHOVEL FOR SCOOPING UP RICE.

6. SLIP STICKS BETWEEN FRONT TEETH AND LOWER LIP FOR "WALRUS FACE" LOOK.

7. ASK FOR FORK.

WHY IT ALWAYS RAINS ON WEEKENDS

Careful study of weather data going back to 19th century confirms what everybody always suspected—rain is much more likely on Saturday and Sunday than during rest of week.

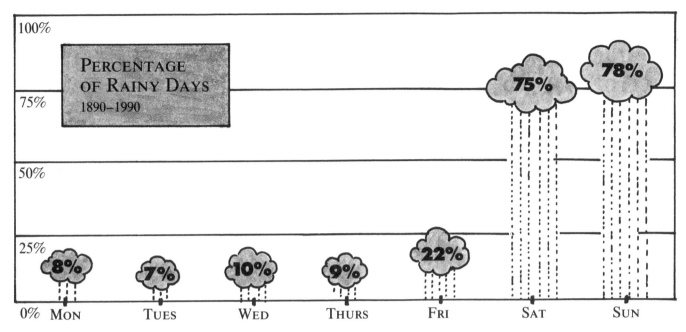

PERCENTAGE OF RAINY DAYS 1890–1990

| MON | TUES | WED | THURS | FRI | SAT | SUN |
| 8% | 7% | 10% | 9% | 22% | 75% | 78% |

Reason for this depressing state of affairs is amazing series of unfortunate geophysical, meteorological, and historical coincidences.

1. Because of the earth's size and speed of its rotation, it takes exactly 4 weeks for a given volume of air to make one complete revolution around globe. Effect of phases of moon on tides sharply reinforces this 28-day cycle.

2. Due to position of major land masses in northern hemisphere and basic west-to-east wind flow of jet stream, Asia is 7 "weather days" from North America, North America is 7 "weather days" from Europe, and Europe is 14 "weather days" from Asia.

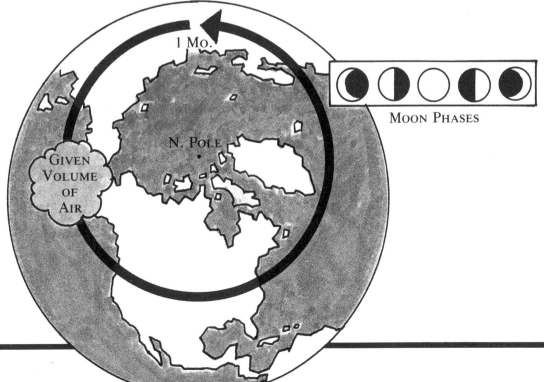

1 Mo.

N. POLE

GIVEN VOLUME OF AIR

MOON PHASES

3. *Thus, if storm that spoiled weekend in Japan stays more or less intact as it crosses the Pacific, it will arrive in time to ruin following weekend for most of U.S., and weekend after that in Britain and on Continent.*

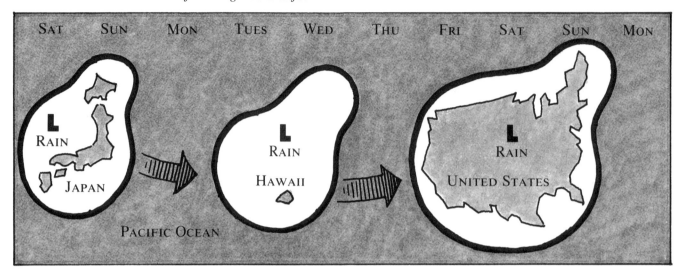

SAT   SUN   MON   TUES   WED   THU   FRI   SAT   SUN   MON

L
RAIN
JAPAN

L
RAIN
HAWAII

L
RAIN
UNITED STATES

PACIFIC OCEAN

4. *And, unlike tropical hurricanes and cyclones, polar storms* do *stay intact over very long periods of time. In fact, climatologists now believe that four basic L.A.T.Z.A.D.U.s (Large-Area Temperate-Zone Atmospheric Disturbance Units), or storms, now circulating in northern latitudes have been essentially unchanged since end of last ice age.*

NEOLITHIC CALENDAR STONE SHOWING WEEKEND PRECIPITATION AND EARLY FORM OF CURSING.

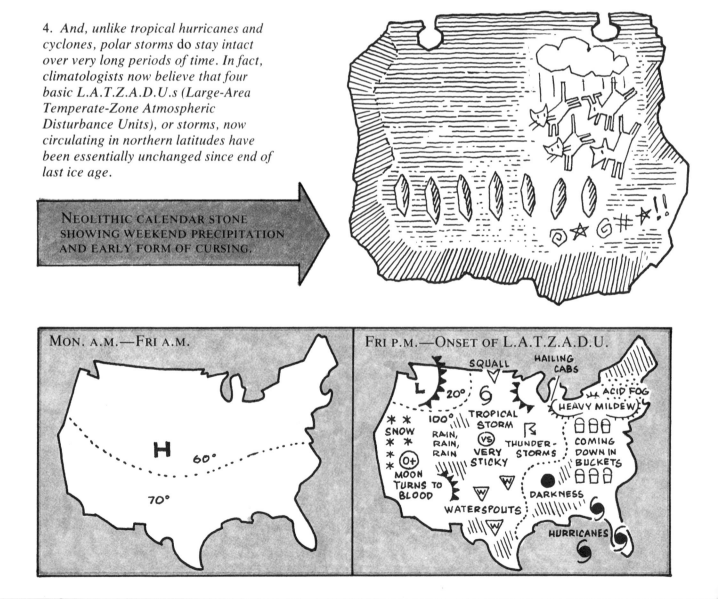

MON. A.M.—FRI A.M.

H
60°
70°

FRI P.M.—ONSET OF L.A.T.Z.A.D.U.

L
20°
SQUALL
HAILING CABS
ACID FOG
HEAVY MILDEW
SNOW
100°
TROPICAL STORM
RAIN, RAIN, RAIN
VS
VERY STICKY
THUNDER-STORMS
COMING DOWN IN BUCKETS
0+
MOON TURNS TO BLOOD
WATERSPOUTS
DARKNESS
HURRICANES

5. *Periodic volcanic eruptions, sunspots, and equinoctial precession should cause storm cycle to "drift" off weekends toward midweek, but widespread industrialization of northern hemisphere promotes cloud formation during week, and custom of closing factories after 5-day work week creates sharp temperature drop, or "thermopause," on Saturday and Sunday that intensifies storms and "locks" them onto weekends. Incredibly enough, weekends themselves are main reason it rains on weekends.*

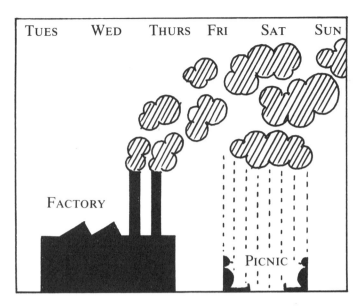

6. *Only way out of dilemma is probably not practical: adoption of new calendar with 9-day weeks, 3-day weekends, and ten 36- or 37- day months. Not only would cost of changeover be immense, but endless squabbles over what to name 2 new days and which months—and hence whose birthdays —to eliminate would undoubtedly doom effort.*

7. *Meanwhile, appearance of telltale Cumulosaturdus clouds on Friday afternoon signals onset of another wet weekend. . . .*

WHY BIG TRUCKS CAN SPEED AND GET AWAY WITH IT

1. *CB radios and conventional radar detectors helped speeding truckers evade arrest, but weren't reliable enough to enable trucking industry to achieve its goal of an average intercity highyway speed of 78 mph.*

2. *In 1982, first of an eventual system of 12 Police Location System (PLS) satellites were launched. Seven are currently in orbit, linked to ground stations in Tulsa, Bakersfield, Spokane, Jacksonville, Dayton, Binghamton, and Chattanooga.*

3. Antennas on virtually all large trucks pick up even weakest signals from speed-detection radar and police-band-radio transmissions and relay them to nearest satellite. Supercomputer instantly incorporates information into nationwide Highway Tracking Report that is updated 400 times per second and broadcast in inaudible digital code by every country and western music station in America as courtesy to truckers. Information is displayed on simple Arrest Risk Data Readout units mounted in truck cabs.

4. When system is fully operational in 1994, average speeds of 95 mph should be possible.

How Recycling Works

1. RECYCLABLES
(FORMERLY GARBAGE)
ARE CAREFULLY SORTED

CLEAR GLASS

BROWN GLASS

GREEN GLASS

CURLERS

WIND-BORNE REDISTRIBUTION
OF RECYCLABLES
TO NEIGHBORING YARDS
AND FARMS

yes!

TOXIC TABLE

GUM, CHEWING

GUM, BUBBLE

PAPER

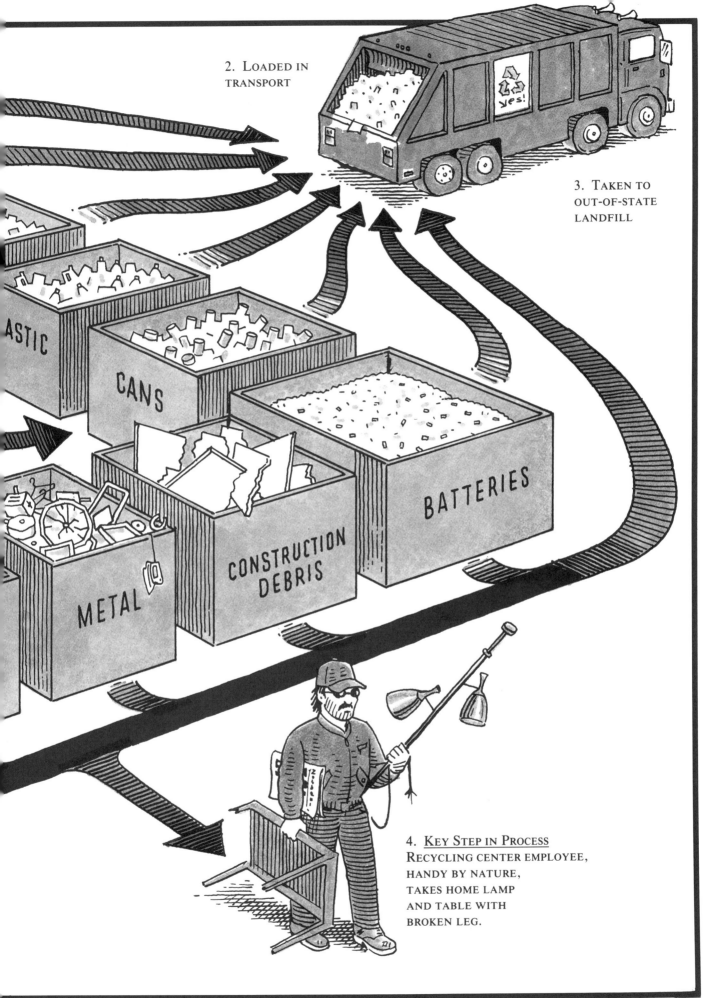

2. LOADED IN TRANSPORT

3. TAKEN TO OUT-OF-STATE LANDFILL

ASTIC

CANS

METAL

CONSTRUCTION DEBRIS

BATTERIES

4. KEY STEP IN PROCESS
RECYCLING CENTER EMPLOYEE, HANDY BY NATURE, TAKES HOME LAMP AND TABLE WITH BROKEN LEG.

HOW NUCLEAR POWER PLANTS WORK

Typical nuclear power plant consists of reactor containment dome, turbine building, control room, phony "cooling tower" with hidden inner chimneys for concealing radioactive leaks in billowing steam clouds, car wash, wet bar, and small movie theater for showing stag films to visiting Nuclear Regulatory Commission inspectors.

SPENT FUEL RODS ARE TEMPORARILY STORED UNDER WATER IN HEAVILY SHIELDED SUBSURFACE CHAMBER NICKNAMED "THE SWIMMING POOL."

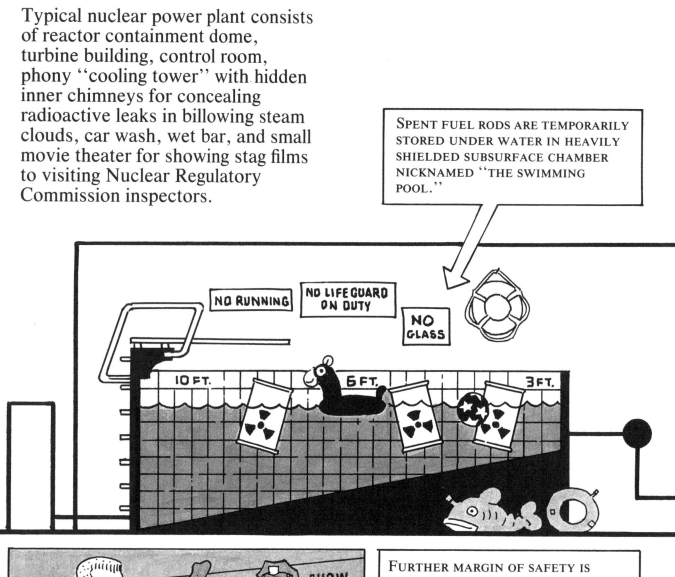

Round-the-clock plant protection is provided by security force of retired high-school crossing guards who patrol complex and check all persons seeking to enter compound for turbans, burnooses, beards, worry beads, copies of the Koran, glassy fanatical stares, falafel breath, tiny cups of coffee, and other key elements of known terrorist profile.

FURTHER MARGIN OF SAFETY IS PROVIDED BY INNER REACTOR VESSEL MADE OF SUPERHARD STAINLESS STEEL ALLOY, BUT LONG-TERM NEUTRON BOMBARDMENT DAMAGES METAL'S MOLECULAR MAKEUP, LEADING TO SERIOUS FORM OF STRUCTURAL WEAKENING CALLED "SWISSIFICATION."

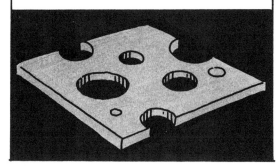

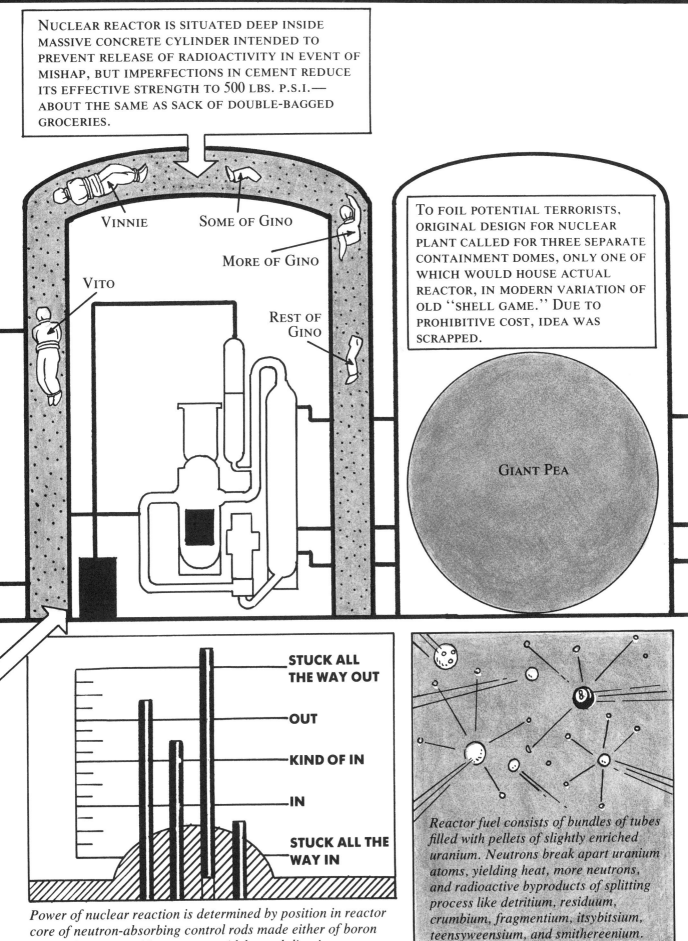

NUCLEAR REACTOR IS SITUATED DEEP INSIDE MASSIVE CONCRETE CYLINDER INTENDED TO PREVENT RELEASE OF RADIOACTIVITY IN EVENT OF MISHAP, BUT IMPERFECTIONS IN CEMENT REDUCE ITS EFFECTIVE STRENGTH TO 500 LBS. P.S.I.— ABOUT THE SAME AS SACK OF DOUBLE-BAGGED GROCERIES.

VINNIE

SOME OF GINO

MORE OF GINO

VITO

REST OF GINO

TO FOIL POTENTIAL TERRORISTS, ORIGINAL DESIGN FOR NUCLEAR PLANT CALLED FOR THREE SEPARATE CONTAINMENT DOMES, ONLY ONE OF WHICH WOULD HOUSE ACTUAL REACTOR, IN MODERN VARIATION OF OLD "SHELL GAME." DUE TO PROHIBITIVE COST, IDEA WAS SCRAPPED.

GIANT PEA

STUCK ALL THE WAY OUT

OUT

KIND OF IN

IN

STUCK ALL THE WAY IN

Power of nuclear reaction is determined by position in reactor core of neutron-absorbing control rods made either of boron or the cheaper, and hence more widely used, licorice.

Reactor fuel consists of bundles of tubes filled with pellets of slightly enriched uranium. Neutrons break apart uranium atoms, yielding heat, more neutrons, and radioactive byproducts of splitting process like detritium, residuum, crumbium, fragmentium, itsybitsium, teensyweensium, and smithereenium.

During fueling and refueling operation, fuel assemblies are inserted into radioactive reactor core by highly paid Hollywood stuntmen dressed in robot costumes.

Thanks to these and other automated remote-control operating systems, entire plant can be run by handful of technicians monitoring impressive array of indicators that constantly report on conditions throughout facility.

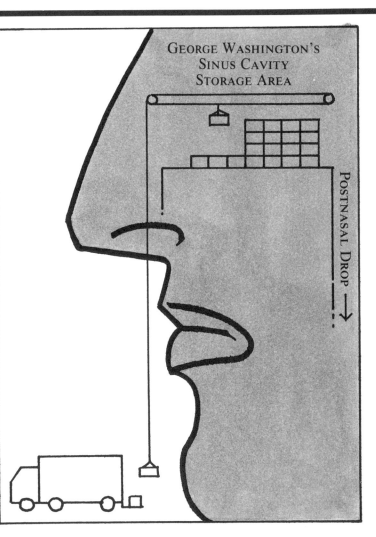

George Washington's
Sinus Cavity
Storage Area

Postnasal Drop →

Because of delays in opening of long-term nuclear waste disposal site, overflow of high-level waste is surreptitiously trucked at night to secret entrance of storage area in hush-hush abandoned bombproof kennels within Mt. Rushmore built during height of cold war to insure survival of pets of high-ranking government officials in event of nuclear attack.

Less severely contaminated materials, like robot suits, protective gear, and pieces of crumbling containment dome are sent for disposal to million-acre site in Alaska rendered unusable when it was divided into one-square-inch lots by cereal companies in 1950s promotional giveaway program.

SUGAR 'NUFFS
LOTS OHO-OIII

FROOTY-TOOTIES
LOTS A191-A216 →

FROOT STONES
LOTS H291-K720

POPS PLUS
LOTS KIII-IIB

PUFFED PUFFIES
LOTS B1013-B4917

KRAZY KRISPIES
LOTS M786-N230 →

CORN WACKIES
LOTS A589-A612 →

FUN FLAKES
LOTS B101-B399 →

BONZ
LOTS

Focus of personnel is always on safety. Comprehensive area-wide evacuation plan is constantly updated and revised.

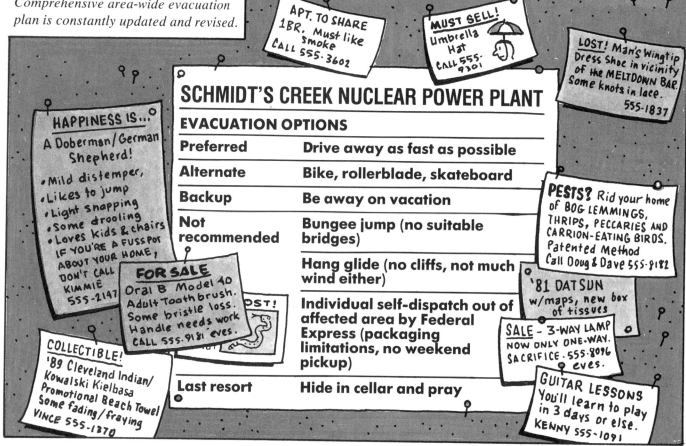

Nuclear plant accidents are unlikely, but the record of past "events" has shown that "weak link" in chain reaction is overheating and even "China Syndrome" melting of reactor core due to drop in water pressure or loss of emergency coolant.

When a plant emergency is declared, siren is immediately sounded and local law enforcement authorities are notified.

Plant personnel quickly fan out to evaluate suitability of potential "receiver communities" at least 100 miles from plant site to house evacuated residents.

Any utility executives in vicinity are contacted by special beepers disguised as digital alarm watches.

As soon as possible, top plant officials hold press conference and issue carefully phrased statement claiming that average dose of radioactivity suffered by populace is equal to one chest X-ray. Statement cleverly fails to mention that X-ray exposure in question is calculated on individual the size of King Kong.

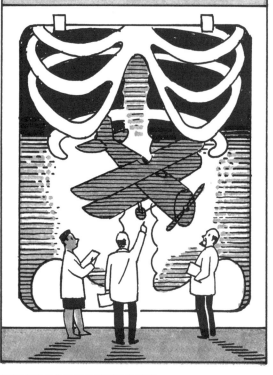

If damaged plant can be repaired in less than 5 years and for under $800,000,000, accident is officially listed as "minor" and temporary adjustment in electric rates pays for cleanup of plant or conversion to conventional electric generating station burning high-sulphur Mexican yellow coal.

Alternatively, if reactor core has actually melted into a hot blob of extremely long-lived and dangerous nuclear byproducts, taxpayers pick up tab for sealing and "mothballing" plant, and note is made somewhere to take a look and see how it is doing sometime in late 25,246 A.D.

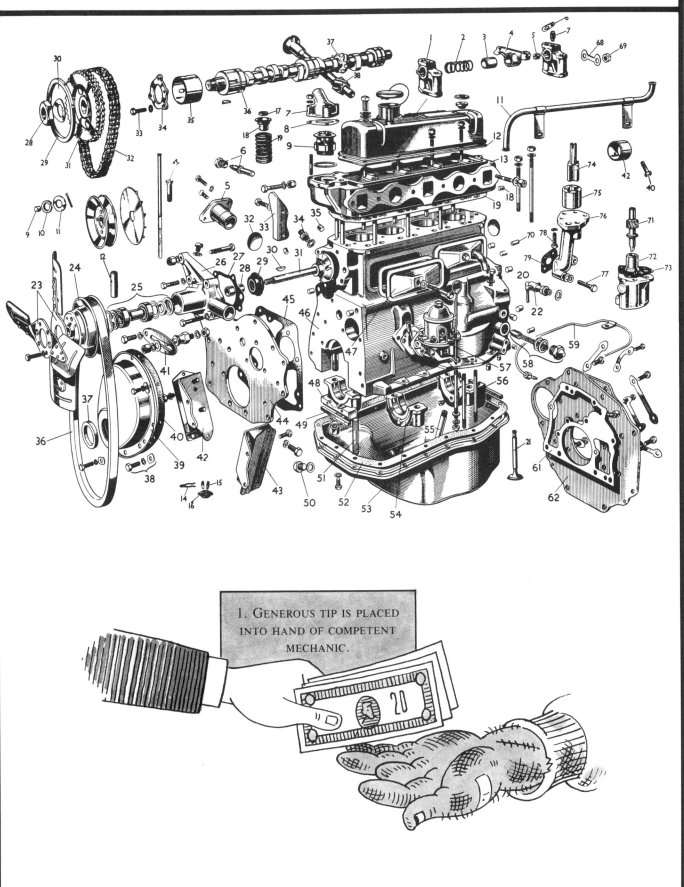

1. Generous tip is placed into hand of competent mechanic.

HOW THE INTERNAL REVENUE SERVICE PICKS PEOPLE FOR AN AUDIT

1. *Days are long past when thousands of IRS auditors had to pore through every return by hand, looking for crudely scrawled insults, obscene doodles, and subtle change in handwritten letter "t" that made checks payable to "Infernal Revenue Service."*

2. *Breakthrough in identifying which taxpayers to put through the wringer came in early 1970s when National Security Agency perfected method of using superfast computers to spot key words—like "secret," "bomb," "dope," and "poison"—used by spies in microwave communications. Now, billions of telephones could be tapped simultaneously in all-out effort to nab enemy agents.*

IRS AGENT SEES COOTIES ON INSIDE FLAP OF ENVELOPE

COOTIES!

NAIL HIM.

MEL-MORT TALENT MANAGEMENT

MURRAY BABY, IT'S NO SECRET—IT'S BOX OFFICE POISON. IT BOMBED IN NEW HAVEN, IT'S GONNA BOMB IN NEW YORK. HEY, I'VE BEEN AN AGENT FOR 30 YEARS, I'M TELLING YA, IT'S THE STRAIGHT DOPE.

3. *Same technique soon permitted automatic optical readers to scan millions of pages of faxes for key written words. In appreciation for taxmen turning blind eye to spooks' enormous deductions for trips to Tahiti to test espionage methods in tropical settings, NSA gave IRS secret technology in 1977.*

WHAT'S THE PASSWORD?

IT WAS AN ITSY-BITSY TEENIE WEENIE

YELLOW POLKA-DOT BIKINI! HEE, HEE, HEE!

4. *IRS quickly adapted sophisticated surveillance system to its needs. By 1980, every radio and TV broadcast in U.S., and most newspapers, magazines, and recently published books were being automatically scanned for every reference to tax-collection that contains such key words as "leeches," "bloodsuckers," "thieves," "highway robbers," and the like. When matches are found, transcript, videotape segment, or page is flashed on computer screen and studied.*

5. *If agents determine that references were derogatory, audit is triggered for everyone involved.*

SOME GUYS JUST NEVER LEARN, DO THEY?

AUDIT LAST 7 (SEVEN) YEARS OF RETURNS OF FOLLOWING TAXPAYERS:

BARRETT, R.

BEARD, H.

BOSWELL, J.

BROWN, P.

CALHOUN, W.

WERNER, M.

HOW JAPANESE RESTAURANTS CAN GET THOSE LITTLE TOWELS HOT ENOUGH TO SCALD YOU WITHOUT HAVING THEM CATCH FIRE OR TURN TO ASH

1. Japanese restaurant hot-towels are precision-woven by robots from space-age ceramic fibers originally developed by NASA as replacement for Space Shuttle tiles. Towels have no absorbent or cleaning qualities, but melting point is higher than that of any known metal.

2. Tightly rolled towels are placed in countertop tokamak deuterium furnace that operates on same principle as high-energy plasma torus used in nuclear-fusion research.

3. Immense pressures and powerful magnetic fields raise temperature of towels to levels found at surface of sun. Waste heat from nuclear reaction is used to stew vats of sukiyaki, fry tempura, and warm little sake bottles.

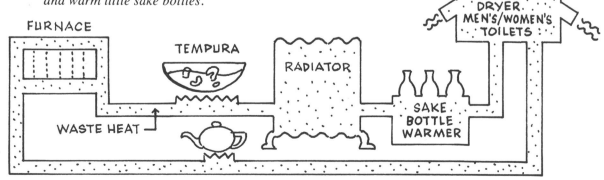

4. *Prepared towels are extracted from reactor by apprentice sushi chefs in sixth stage of arduous, Zen-like "Way of the Fish" training—mastery of key "Show Me Match That Burns Twice" ritual.*

5. *Towels are carried from kitchen on special trays fabricated from lightweight fire-bricks. Hostesses—protected by kimonos of heat-resistant carbon fabrics usually worn by professional oil-well fire fighters—use special tungsten tongs to serve towels.*

6. *Amazing towel material gives up its heat instantly, turning into cold, clammy rag in less than 5 seconds. Slightly slimy feel is residue of neutron-rich heavy water used in fusion reaction.*

How Dry Cleaners Put Your Suit Jacket with Someone Else's Pants or Skirt

CLOTHING CLOVERLEAF
EVERY 3RD AND 8TH GARMENT IS SENT IN AN EAST-WEST DIRECTION. ASSURES LACK OF NUMERICAL AND CHRONOLOGICAL ORDER.

THE RANDOMIZER
(HUMAN INEPTITUDE SIMULATOR) REMOVES EVERY 4TH ODD-NUMBERED SUIT AND SWITCHES PANTS WITH EVERY 7TH EVEN-NUMBERED SUIT.

WHY SCALES SAY YOU WEIGH MORE THAN YOU KNOW YOU DO

Unable to raise prices during deep recession, top consumer-goods industry leaders decide to shrink products instead. In unannounced meeting with high-ranking members of Nixon Administration, these major campaign contributors ask for —and get—agreement to secretly "devalue" ounce by 5 percent. Pound will seem the same, but will actually weigh only 15.1 ounces.

It is decided only common household purchases will be affected and that adjustment will be phased in over two-year period starting in July 1973 in order to hide shrinkage of popular products.

Critical to program's success is adoption of new weight standard by commercial scale industry. Promises of huge classified defense contracts convince nation's scale manufacturers to go along.

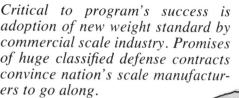

PROJECT PONDEROSA

CONSTRUCTION OF $1 BILLION SCA IN MOJAVE DESERT TO DETERMI WHETHER MINUTE CHANGES IN WEIGH OF A TRILLION TONS OF SAND CAN USED TO DETECT TINY GRAVITATION VARIATIONS CAUSED BY TRANSIT ENEMY SPY SATELLITES.

HOW AN ELECTRIC SHAVER WORKS

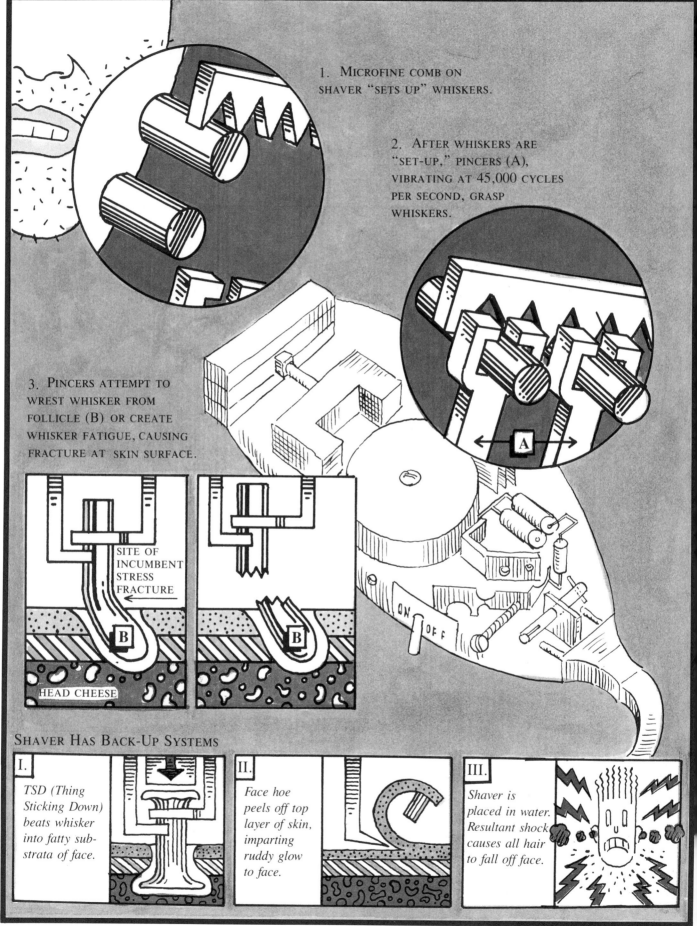

1. MICROFINE COMB ON SHAVER "SETS UP" WHISKERS.

2. AFTER WHISKERS ARE "SET-UP," PINCERS (A), VIBRATING AT 45,000 CYCLES PER SECOND, GRASP WHISKERS.

3. PINCERS ATTEMPT TO WREST WHISKER FROM FOLLICLE (B) OR CREATE WHISKER FATIGUE, CAUSING FRACTURE AT SKIN SURFACE.

A

SITE OF INCUMBENT STRESS FRACTURE

B

B

HEAD CHEESE

ON OFF

SHAVER HAS BACK-UP SYSTEMS

I.

TSD (Thing Sticking Down) beats whisker into fatty sub-strata of face.

II.

Face hoe peels off top layer of skin, imparting ruddy glow to face.

III.

Shaver is placed in water. Resultant shock causes all hair to fall off face.

How Important Economic Decisions Are Made

1. Every 90 days, top Federal Reserve officials study leading economic indicators for clues on how economy is doing.

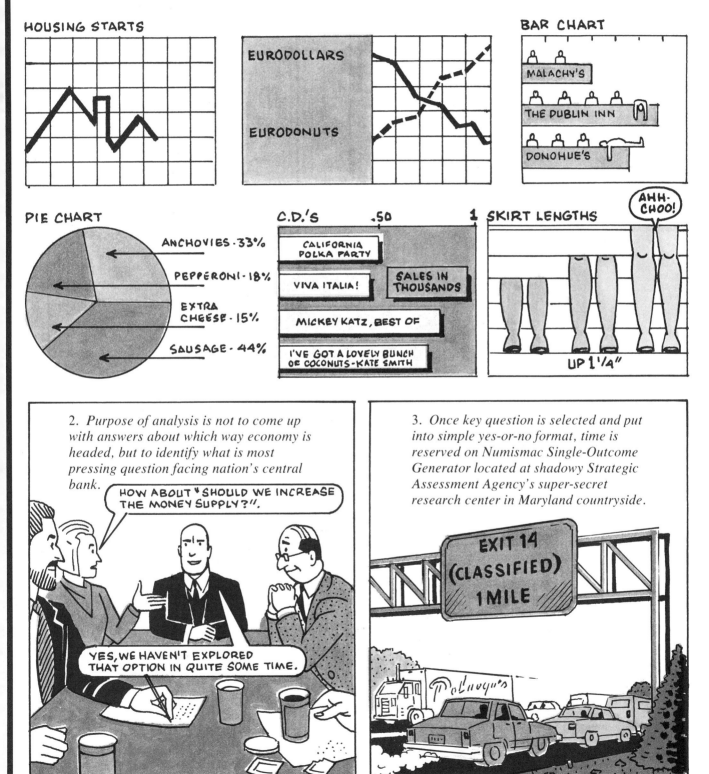

HOUSING STARTS

EURODOLLARS

EURODONUTS

BAR CHART

MALACHY'S

THE DUBLIN INN

DONOHUE'S

PIE CHART

ANCHOVIES · 33%

PEPPERONI · 18%

EXTRA CHEESE · 15%

SAUSAGE · 44%

C.D.'S   .50   1

CALIFORNIA POLKA PARTY

VIVA ITALIA!

SALES IN THOUSANDS

MICKEY KATZ, BEST OF

I'VE GOT A LOVELY BUNCH OF COCONUTS - KATE SMITH

SKIRT LENGTHS

AHH-CHOO!

UP 1 1/4"

2. *Purpose of analysis is not to come up with answers about which way economy is headed, but to identify what is most pressing question facing nation's central bank.*

HOW ABOUT "SHOULD WE INCREASE THE MONEY SUPPLY?".

YES, WE HAVEN'T EXPLORED THAT OPTION IN QUITE SOME TIME.

3. *Once key question is selected and put into simple yes-or-no format, time is reserved on Numismac Single-Outcome Generator located at shadowy Strategic Assessment Agency's super-secret research center in Maryland countryside.*

EXIT 14 (CLASSIFIED) 1 MILE

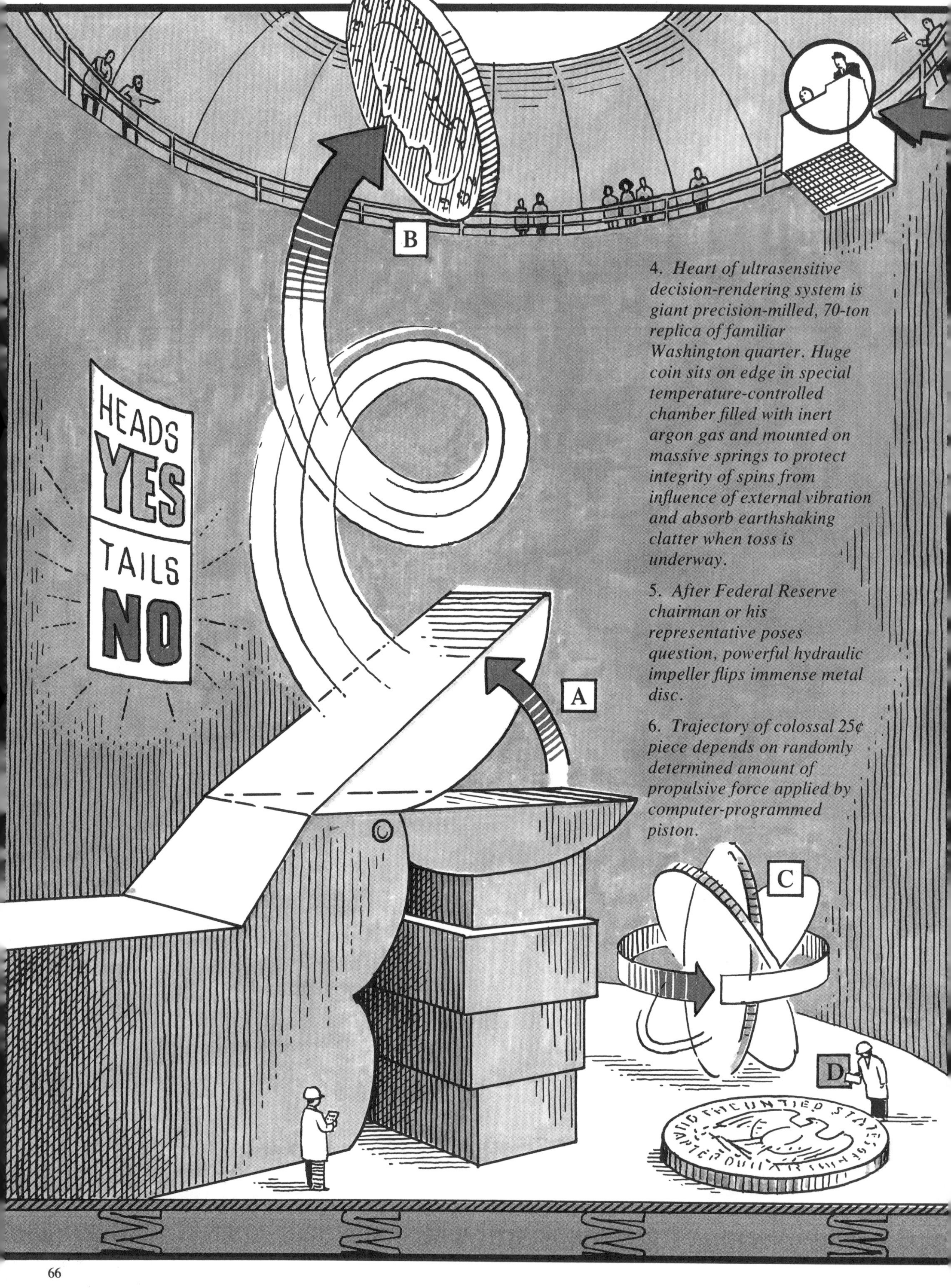

HEADS
YES
TAILS
NO

B

A

C

D

4. *Heart of ultrasensitive decision-rendering system is giant precision-milled, 70-ton replica of familiar Washington quarter. Huge coin sits on edge in special temperature-controlled chamber filled with inert argon gas and mounted on massive springs to protect integrity of spins from influence of external vibration and absorb earthshaking clatter when toss is underway.*

5. *After Federal Reserve chairman or his representative poses question, powerful hydraulic impeller flips immense metal disc.*

6. *Trajectory of colossal 25¢ piece depends on randomly determined amount of propulsive force applied by computer-programmed piston.*

7. *Since it takes nearly eight hours to raise and re-erect Gyrovariant Alternative Indicator for next toss, Numismac is reserved for questions of greatest national importance. Highest priority is held by White House, Pentagon, CIA, State Dept., and National Weather Service in hurricane season. Economists get access only every 3 months.*

8. *This explains why major policy changes are announced no more than four times a year.*

9. *Carefully phrased reference to "quarter" always gets big laugh back at Federal Reserve building.*

WHY THINGS WON'T FIT BACK IN THE BOXES THEY CAME IN

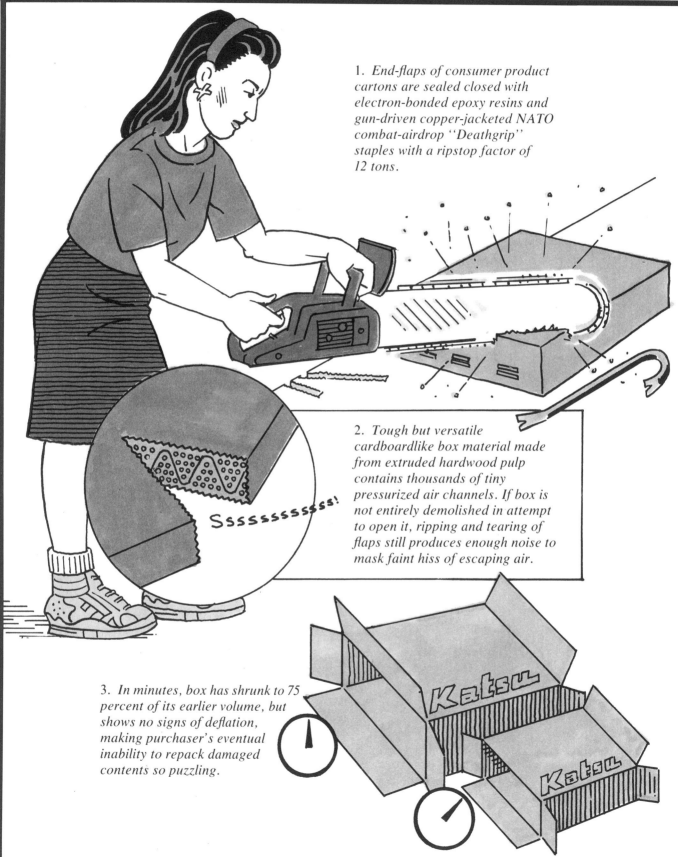

1. *End-flaps of consumer product cartons are sealed closed with electron-bonded epoxy resins and gun-driven copper-jacketed NATO combat-airdrop "Deathgrip" staples with a ripstop factor of 12 tons.*

2. *Tough but versatile cardboardlike box material made from extruded hardwood pulp contains thousands of tiny pressurized air channels. If box is not entirely demolished in attempt to open it, ripping and tearing of flaps still produces enough noise to mask faint hiss of escaping air.*

Sssssssssss!

3. *In minutes, box has shrunk to 75 percent of its earlier volume, but shows no signs of deflation, making purchaser's eventual inability to repack damaged contents so puzzling.*

Katsu

Katsu

4. *As further obstacle to repacking, photosensitive styrofoam inserts made of Photofoam® gradually expand when exposed to ordinary daylight. Although they retain their shape, within an hour they nearly double in size.*

5. AN IRONIC FOOTNOTE: *For many industries, packing process is a vicious circle. Effort to ship goods in impossible-to-open boxes into which damaged products cannot be reinserted for return to manufacturer is actually responsible for most defects in consumer items.*

LOADER—DROPS PRODUCT INTO STYROFOAM PACKING

STITCHER

RAMMER— INSERTS PACKED PRODUCT INTO SHIPPING CARTON

ADHESIVE

HOW TERRORISTS GET THEIR GUNS THROUGH AIRPORT SECURITY SYSTEMS

REEE! REEE!

2. *Carry-on items are put through separate inspection process in which they are X-rayed, but not specifically tested for metal content. Distracted by incessant buzz of metal detector and annoying whoops of hand-held electronic screening devices used in body searches, security personnel monitoring X-ray screen fail to notice subtle alterations in appearance of familiar travelers' articles.*

ART POSTERS

Candy

1. *To impress public with thoroughness of preflight precautions, airlines set walk-through metal-detection equipment to maximum sensitivity. Alarm is triggered by metallic objects as small as set of luggage keys or rolled-up ball of gum foil.*

How They Come up with Ads

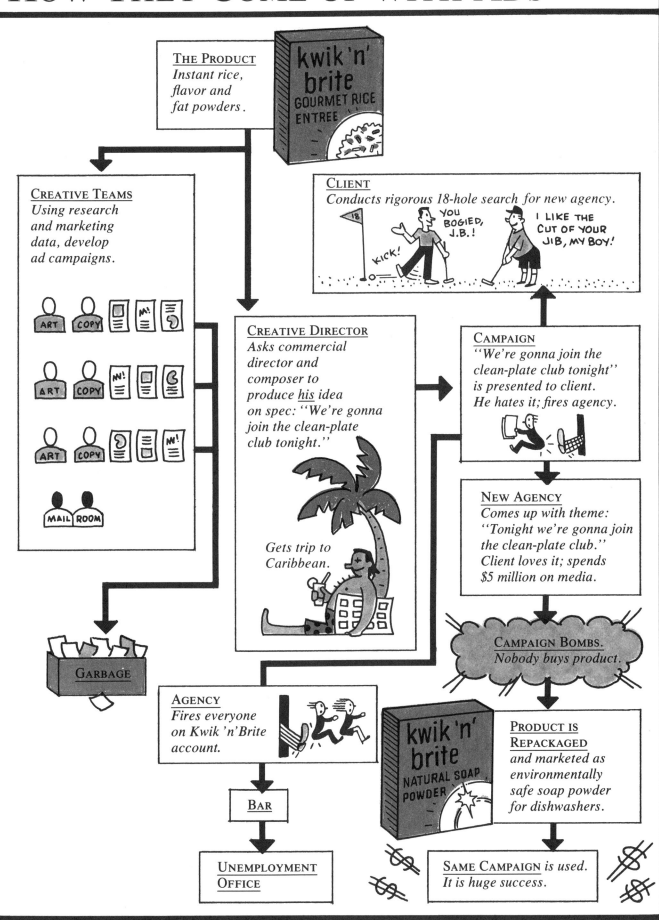

The Product
Instant rice, flavor and fat powders.

kwik 'n' brite GOURMET RICE ENTREE

Creative Teams
Using research and marketing data, develop ad campaigns.

ART COPY
ART COPY
ART COPY
MAIL ROOM

Client
Conducts rigorous 18-hole search for new agency.

KICK! YOU BOGIED, J.B.!
I LIKE THE CUT OF YOUR JIB, MY BOY!

Creative Director
Asks commercial director and composer to produce his idea on spec: "We're gonna join the clean-plate club tonight."

Gets trip to Caribbean.

Campaign
"We're gonna join the clean-plate club tonight" is presented to client. He hates it; fires agency.

New Agency
Comes up with theme: "Tonight we're gonna join the clean-plate club." Client loves it; spends $5 million on media.

Garbage

Campaign Bombs.
Nobody buys product.

Agency
Fires everyone on Kwik 'n' Brite account.

kwik 'n' brite NATURAL SOAP POWDER

Product is Repackaged
and marketed as environmentally safe soap powder for dishwashers.

Bar

Unemployment Office

Same Campaign *is used. It is huge success.*

Why Constellations Don't Look Anything at all Like What They're Named After

Because of huge increase in atmospheric pollution since beginning of industrial age, even on clearest night less than one-fifth of stars formerly visible in ancient times can be seen with naked eye today.

2,000 B.C.

LITTLE HORSE (EQUULEUS)

WATER CARRIER (AQUARIUS)

GOAT (CAPRICORNUS)

SOUTHERN FISH (PISCIS AUSTRINUS)

LATE 20TH CENTURY A.D.

Little Horse (Equuleus)

Water Carrier (Aquarius)

Goat (Capricornus)

Southern Fish (Piscis Austrinus)

WHY PLASTIC WRAP ALWAYS HAS TO BE THROWN OUT LONG BEFORE THE ROLL IS USED UP

In early 1960s, scientists at leading chemical company try to produce super-brittle plastic to make it virtually impossible to pry open battery compartments of transistor radios without breaking off piece of cover. Instead, they stumble on new miracle compound they call "Phenomenyl."

BETTER LIVING THROUGH PHENOMENYL

FATHER OF PHENOMENYL

Amazing synthetic resin could be extruded into thin, incredibly strong sheets of transparent plastic film that clung naturally to bowls, jar tops, leftovers—anything—and yet was easy to peel from roll.

PHENOMENYL® TURNS TONIGHT'S SCRAPS INTO TOMORROW'S DINNER!

PIE

MEATLOAF

SALT AND PEPPER

COFFEE

Product implementation specialists quickly found that one $1.29 roll would last family of four for two years and nixed further development. Attempt was made to use new plastic for unopenable blister packs, but compound was shelved after perfection of Chem-Lok® bulletproof acrylic packaging.

BLISTER-PAK

WATER JACKET

30 CAL. WATER-COOLED MACHINE GUN

A year later, second research group working on project to shorten life and reduce durability of suddenly fashionable shiny vinyl women's boots, jackets, and miniskirts discovers key additive that will weaken almost any plastic.

NOW, WITH FRAGYL® ADDED

Meanwhile, original team, now engaged in long-term program to make grease, grime, and soap residue adhere better to plastic shower curtains to hasten replacement cycle comes up with method of endowing any plastic with permanent powerful static-electric charge.

These two breakthroughs breathe new life into Phenomenyl. Plastic wrap can now be manufactured in version that tears easily and sticks to itself, so roll has to be thrown out third of the way through when futile effort to locate and grasp leading edge of plastic film results in hopeless snarl of impossibly tangled and tattered strips.

UNEXPECTED BONUS: *ROLLS OF TEAR-OFF PLASTIC BAGS FOR PRODUCE SECTIONS OF SUPERMARKETS WITH NO OPEN END!*

Open other end

Open other end

WHY TOASTERS EITHER JUST WARM THE BREAD OR BURN IT TO A CRISP

Whether modern plastic model or old-fashioned chrome beauty, all toasters work on the same basic principle.

1. *Inside toaster housing are two separate cooking elements, neither of which can be adjusted. Knob or switch for setting desired darkness of toast is a dummy.*

NICHROME HEATING WIRE

RHODIUM FLASH SCREEN

CAPACITOR

DUMMY DARKNESS KNOB

LT · DK

2. *When bread is placed in slot and slide lever is depressed first time, low-power nichrome heating wire emits .05 microtherms of radiant heat—about enough to warm the wings of a moth. Telltale "Sing-Sing hot seat" light-dimming effect is not caused by dully glowing visible heating element drawing power, but capacitor in base of toaster storing electricity for later discharge.*

3. *When uncooked bread pops up and slide lever of toaster is depressed second time, capacitor sends 10,000-volt electric charge into rhodium flash screen on inner wall of toaster. Bread is bathed in 10-second kilojoule blast of invisible far-infrared heat energy and is instantly carbonized.*

4. *Unmistakable odor of incinerated bakery product signals that toast is ready.*

HOT SEAT EFFECT

ON · OFF

FRENCH USE CARBONIZED BREAD (PAIN CHARBONÉE) FOR PORTRAITURE

WHY JURY DUTY IS SUCH A PAIN IN THE ASS

1. *Names of prospective jurors are taken from lists of registered voters and licensed drivers, but final selection is based on information obtained from supposedly confidential tax returns.*

2. *Ideal juror is self-employed entrepreneur, high-ranking corporate manager, or busy professional—in short, someone who hates to waste time.*

3. *Although plea bargaining in criminal cases and out-of-court settlements of civil suits have eliminated vast majority of actual trials, thousands of people still get jury summonses each week.*

4. *After reporting to courthouse, pool of potential jurors spends two weeks reading novels and doing crosswords in noisy, smelly, cramped, poorly lit, windowless assembly room with only one working pay phone.*

5. *Very few people are ever sent to a courtroom for voir dire examination. Those who do get called are immediately disqualified for no apparent reason.*

6. *Process seems designed solely to make large numbers of people boiling mad. Oddly enough, this is in fact whole purpose of jury-duty system.*

7. *Heat from furious jurors doing a slow burn is drawn out of juror assembly room through ceiling vents. Piped through hot-air ducts, it keeps entire courthouse complex toasty warm even on coldest days.*

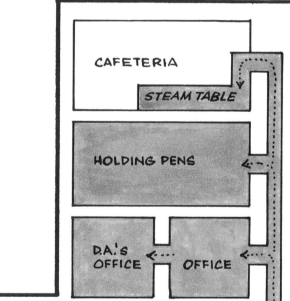

8. *Scheme is as efficient as it is ingenious. Few jurors are summoned in summer months, and requests for 6-month postponement of service are always granted between Memorial Day and Labor Day, but routinely denied at all other times.*

9. *Paltry per diem payments to citizens for jury service are tiny fraction of millions of dollars saved in annual heating bills. Money is used to decorate rarely seen judges' chambers and send courthouse personnel to legal conferences in pricey resorts.*

WHY AIR CONDITIONERS KEEP YOU AWAKE ALL NIGHT

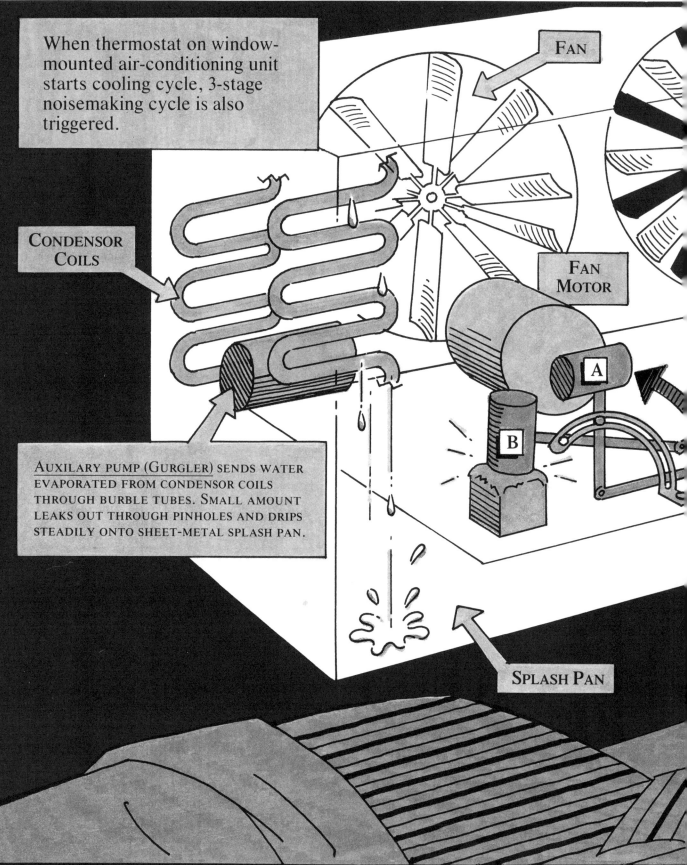

When thermostat on window-mounted air-conditioning unit starts cooling cycle, 3-stage noisemaking cycle is also triggered.

FAN

CONDENSOR COILS

FAN MOTOR

A

B

AUXILARY PUMP (GURGLER) SENDS WATER EVAPORATED FROM CONDENSOR COILS THROUGH BURBLE TUBES. SMALL AMOUNT LEAKS OUT THROUGH PINHOLES AND DRIPS STEADILY ONTO SHEET-METAL SPLASH PAN.

SPLASH PAN

WHY YOU NEVER WIN THE STATE LOTTERY

1. *You choose from these numbers to make your Lucky Lotto pick:*

YOUR ADDRESS   YOUR INSEAM

YOUR BIRTHDAY

LUCKY LOTTO
We had 10$ milloin winer lest wik! $ $ $

2. *Completed ticket is presented to agent, who carefully enters your selection into computer.*

3. *Your Lucky Lotto number enters fiber-optic network. (Note similarity to celery stalk.)*

SEE?

362156

362156

4. *Number is beamed to state capital.*

VIRTVE

362156

PIGEON NESTING AREA

5. *Number enters mainframe of state's massive computer along with names of tax and traffic law violators.*

ENTIRE PROCESS IS SUPERVISED BY THE GOVERNOR.

LUCKY LOTTO

6. *At precisely 10:30 P.M., a woman, personally selected by the governor for her physical beauty, spins a basketful of numbered Ping-Pong balls.*

7. *Escape mechanism allows 7 balls to roll onto track for viewing by TV audiences.*

7a. *The ball with your winning number is borrowed by the governor's children for their own games of chance.*

FWOK!

SLAM!

How Pocket Knives Work

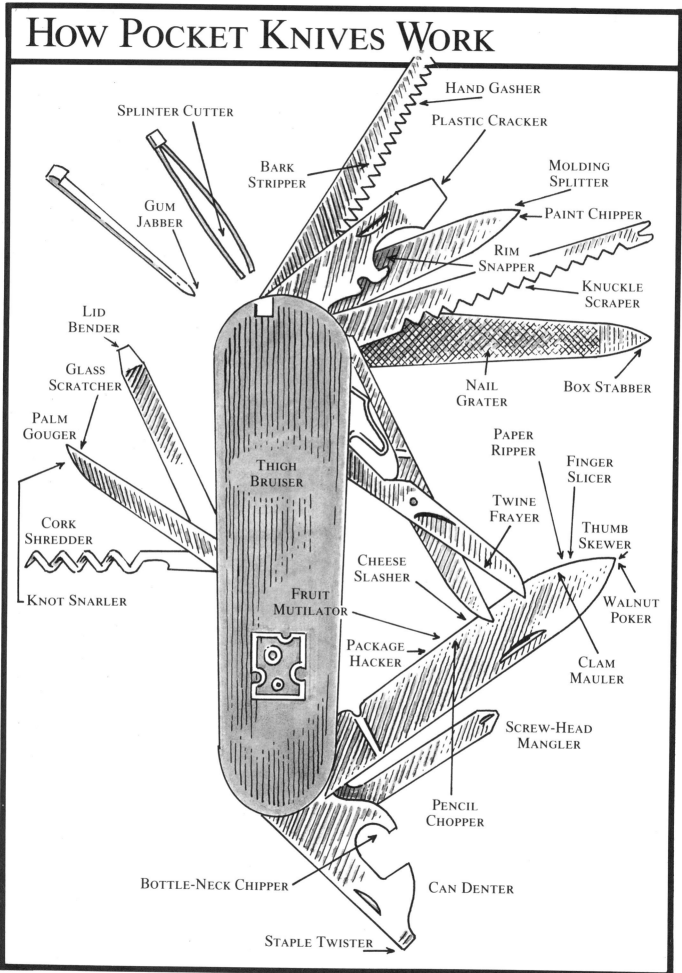

SPLINTER CUTTER

GUM JABBER

HAND GASHER

PLASTIC CRACKER

BARK STRIPPER

MOLDING SPLITTER

PAINT CHIPPER

RIM SNAPPER

KNUCKLE SCRAPER

LID BENDER

GLASS SCRATCHER

PALM GOUGER

NAIL GRATER

BOX STABBER

CORK SHREDDER

KNOT SNARLER

THIGH BRUISER

PAPER RIPPER

FINGER SLICER

TWINE FRAYER

THUMB SKEWER

CHEESE SLASHER

FRUIT MUTILATOR

WALNUT POKER

PACKAGE HACKER

CLAM MAULER

SCREW-HEAD MANGLER

PENCIL CHOPPER

BOTTLE-NECK CHIPPER

CAN DENTER

STAPLE TWISTER

WHY WINDOWS JAM

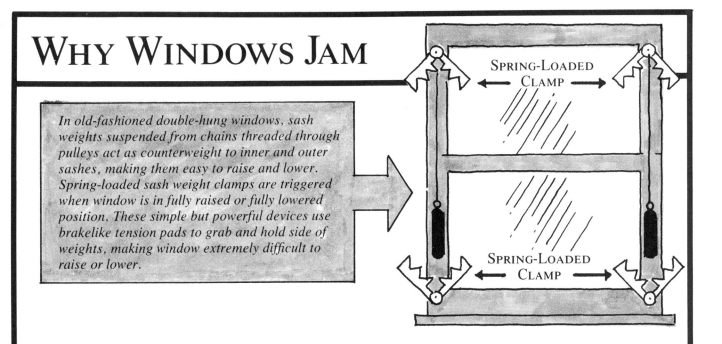

In old-fashioned double-hung windows, sash weights suspended from chains threaded through pulleys act as counterweight to inner and outer sashes, making them easy to raise and lower. Spring-loaded sash weight clamps are triggered when window is in fully raised or fully lowered position. These simple but powerful devices use brakelike tension pads to grab and hold side of weights, making window extremely difficult to raise or lower.

SPRING-LOADED CLAMP

SPRING-LOADED CLAMP

In modern windows, which have no counterweight mechanism and depend on tight friction of metal slides to keep window sash in desired position, a more sophisticated and ingenious system is employed. Two flat, heat-sensitive, bimetallic strips are installed behind window tracks. In warm weather, lower end of strips deforms inward with progressive force as temperature rises above 64°, pinching frame and making window almost impossible to open. Once window is opened, and temperatures drop below 64°, lower end relaxes and upper end deforms inward, making window extremely difficult to close.

Although in both cases deformation is very slight—less than a centimeter—it is more than enough to severely jam even smoothest-operating window owing to small tolerances of snug-fitting window tracks.

CUTAWAY SHOWING BIMETALLIC STRIPS

WHY YOUR SNAPSHOTS ALWAYS COME OUT LOUSY

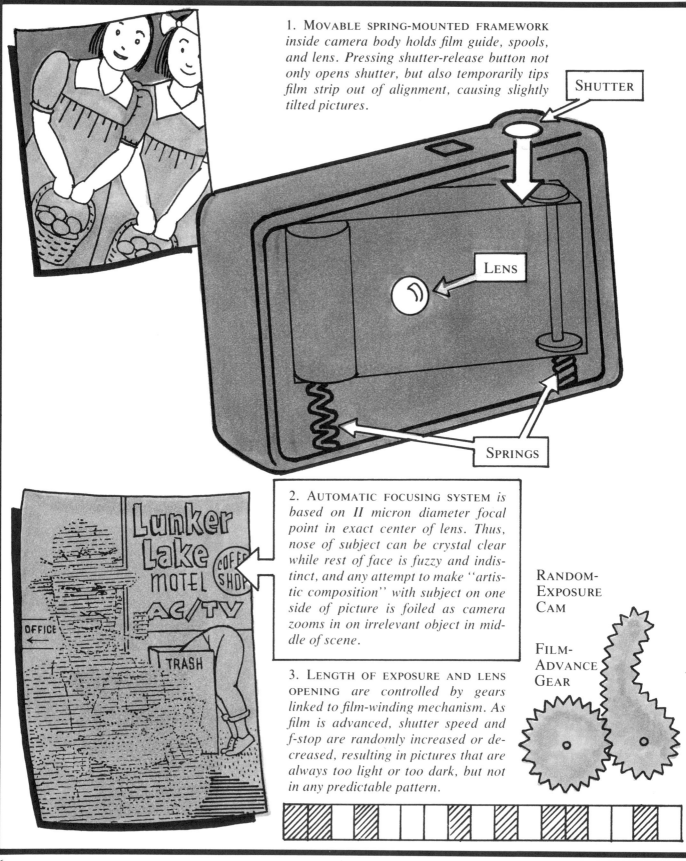

1. MOVABLE SPRING-MOUNTED FRAMEWORK *inside camera body holds film guide, spools, and lens. Pressing shutter-release button not only opens shutter, but also temporarily tips film strip out of alignment, causing slightly tilted pictures.*

SHUTTER

LENS

SPRINGS

2. AUTOMATIC FOCUSING SYSTEM *is based on II micron diameter focal point in exact center of lens. Thus, nose of subject can be crystal clear while rest of face is fuzzy and indistinct, and any attempt to make "artistic composition" with subject on one side of picture is foiled as camera zooms in on irrelevant object in middle of scene.*

RANDOM-EXPOSURE CAM

FILM-ADVANCE GEAR

3. LENGTH OF EXPOSURE AND LENS OPENING *are controlled by gears linked to film-winding mechanism. As film is advanced, shutter speed and f-stop are randomly increased or decreased, resulting in pictures that are always too light or too dark, but not in any predictable pattern.*

PREFLASH

MAIN FLASH

4. **FLASHBULB FILAMENT** *produces two separate flashes. Preflash is triggered* $\frac{1}{2}$ *second before main flash, insuring that subjects have tightly closed eyes and weird grimaces when actual photo is taken.*

5. **MAIN FLASH** *emits same harsh bluish light used in police station line-ups, emphasizing wrinkles and causing overexposed washed-out "mug shot" look and creepy red "vampire eyes."*

6. **CAMERA LENS** *has subtle built-in optical flaw similar to distortion in fun-house mirrors. Slight horizontal deflection makes people seem fatter than they really are without producing noticeable lateral bulge in landscapes and inanimate objects.*

7. *Effect is greatly enhanced when enlargements are made.*

How Taxi Meters Work

Everyone agrees that taxi drivers drive much too fast, always seem to head right for deepest potholes, slam on brakes and lean on horns at every opportunity, and talk incessantly during entire hair-raising ride. But no one knows real reason for demented behavior—design of taxi meters dictates that cab must be operated in completely insane manner in order to obtain maximum fare.

Taxi meters calculate fare four ways. Contrary to popular belief, elapsed time and miles traveled have no effect whatsoever on final charge for trip.

YOU SLAM DOOR, I'LL SLAM YOU. -Driver

YOU LISTEN TO ME! -Driver

NO EATING, EXCEPT FOR DRIVER, HE CAN EAT.

COMPLAINT? Tell those jerks in Washington

Rose o' th' Road FRESHN'R

AUXILIARY PRESSURE PAD

3.

1. VERTICAL MOTION SENSOR *records distance body of cab travels up and down as it bounces over uneven pavement surfaces. Heart of system is "Shakometer" adapted from earthquake-recording devices that socks rider 10¢ for every 20 feet of perpendicular movement, and 15¢ every time any single jolt exceeds 500 foot-pounds of rebound force— about enough to dislodge a tooth filling.*

1.

1.38 FT

4. ACOUSTICATOR on side of meter box is activated by noises detected inside cab. Ear-splitting blasts of horn, heated statement of political views by loudmouthed driver, and high-volume din from cab radio are all charged to passenger at basic rate of one penny per decibel-minute.

2. VELOCIMETER attached by cable to speedometer translates miles per hour into cents per miles per hour. Thus the faster you go, the more it costs.

3. DECELEROMETER monitors number and intensity of sudden stops and front- and rear-end impacts. Brake-slams are 25¢ each; fender-benders are 50¢. Auxiliary pressure pad in cab's back seat also adds a nickel to fare every time passenger's body is lifted entirely off seat by unexpected driving maneuvers.

WHY DRINKING FOUNTAINS EITHER DRIBBLE OR SQUIRT

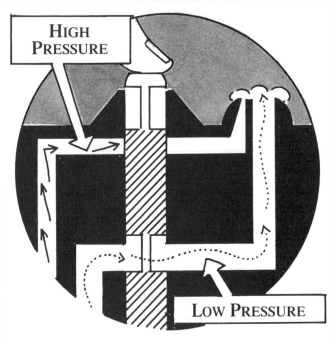

HIGH PRESSURE

LOW PRESSURE

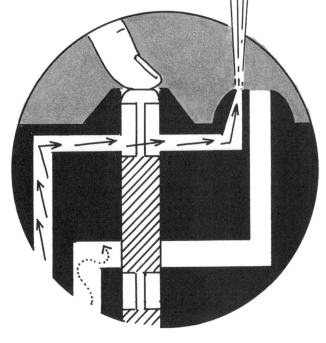

1. WHEN PUSHED DOWN, SPRING-LOADED TAP LETS WATER BUBBLE OUT, THEN GRADUALLY REDUCES FLOW FROM A SLOW DRIBBLE TO A DROOL AS BUTTON IS PRESSED DOWN FURTHER.

2. AS THIRSTY INDIVIDUAL LEANS FORWARD TO CATCH SLIGHT TRICKLE FROM OUTLET, AND INSTINCTIVELY CONTINUES TO APPLY INCREASING PRESSURE TO BUTTON, DESCENDING PISTON SUDDENLY OPENS HIGH PRESSURE WATER LINE, RELEASING POWERFUL SPRAY.